WALL STREET, BANKS, AND AMERICAN FOREIGN POLICY

Wall Street, Banks, and American Foreign Policy

Second Edition

By

Murray N. Rothbard

With Introductions by
Anthony Gregory and Justin Raimondo

First appeared in World Market Perspective *(1984) and later
under the same title as a monograph produced by the
Center for Libertarian Studies (1995)*

Ludwig
von Mises
Institute
AUBURN, ALABAMA

Ludwig von Mises Institute
518 West Magnolia Avenue
Auburn, Alabama 36832
mises.org

Large Print Edition published 2012 by Skyler J. Collins.
Visit: www.skylerjcollins.com

Cover image by StockFreeImages.com.

ISBN-13: 978-1479396825
ISBN-10: 1479396826

Contents

Introduction to the 2011 Edition

By Anthony Gregory

The idea that corporate interests, banking elites and politicians conspire to set U.S. policy is at once obvious and beyond the pale. Everyone knows that the military-industrial complex is fat and corrupt, that presidents bestow money and privilege on their donors and favored businesses, that a revolving door connects Wall Street and the White House, that economic motivations lurk behind America's wars. But to make too fine a point of this is typically dismissed as unserious conspiracy theorizing, unworthy of mainstream consideration.

We have seen this paradox at work in the aftermath of the 2008 financial collapse. The left-liberals blame Wall Street and Big Finance for betraying the masses out of predatory greed and for being rewarded for their irresponsibility by Washington's bailouts. At the same time, the left appears reluctant to oppose these bailouts outright, seeing the spending as a necessary evil to return the global economy to stability, however inequitably. What's more, left-liberals fail to call out President Obama and Democratic leaders for their undeniable hand in all this. They blame Goldman-Sachs but see their president, who got more campaign money from the firm than from almost any other source, as a helpless victim of circumstance, rather than an energetic conspirator in corporate malfeasance on top of being the enthusiastic heir and expansionist of George W. Bush's aggressive foreign policy.

The Tea Party right is also hesitant to examine the corporate state too closely. These conservatives detect an elitism in Obama's governance but are loath to earnestly challenge the economic status quo, for it would lead to uncomfortable questions about the warfare state, defense contractors, U.S. wars, the whole history of the Republican Party, and all the typical rightwing assumptions about the inherent fairness of America's supposedly "free enterprise" system. By refusing to admit that economic fundamentals were unsound through the entirety of the Bush years—by failing to acknowledge the imperial reality of U.S. wars and their debilitating effect on the average household budget—the right is forgoing its chance to delve beyond the surface in its criticism of Obama's reign.

Many on the right call Obama a "socialist" as many on the left accused Bush of being a "fascist," neither group seeing the stark similarities in almost all of their policies. Meanwhile, the more mainstream forces on both left and right refuse to countenance such "extremist" rhetoric and insist that both political parties, for all their differences, have the best of America's interests at heart. In the left's unflinching loyalty to social democracy and economic intervention and the right's invincible love for the military and support for corporate America we see why we are allowed to decry corruption and special interests, but not dig too much deeper than that, lest we be relegated to the periphery of respectable discussion.

Never afraid to slaughter sacred cows, Murray N. Rothbard goes far beyond the mainstream lamentations in his trenchant *Wall Street, Banks, and American Foreign Policy*. He analyzes over a century of U.S. militarism and corporate cronyism, naming names, sparing no one, and demonstrating the continuity of imperialism regardless of the party in control, alongside the many overlapping and competing business interests behind the curtains. Rothbard's account of the clash between the Morgans and Rockefellers, who had some interests in common and some in conflict, brilliantly hones in on the complexity of the story while also explaining generally the dynamics of power. The discussion of the "Cowboy" firms of the West (and their representatives in Washington) vs. the "Yankee" Northeastern Establishment is similarly illuminating: "While both groups favor the Cold War, the Cowboys are more nationalistic, more hawkish, and less inclined to worry about what our European allies are thinking.... It should be clear that the name of the political party in power is far less important than the particular regime's financial and banking connections."

This fantastic written work is the definitive answer to many naysayers—those who boast great differences between Republicans and Democrats; those who insist the main engine behind U.S. wars is concern for national defense or human rights abroad; those who dismiss "conspiracy theorizing" as oversimplified accusations of behind-the-scenes power-broking, devoid of nuance and sophistication; and those who myopically think all major decisions are made by the exact same clique of major players, rather than through a complicated confluence of sundry interests and forces.

Peddlers of oversimplified conspiracy theories will be uncomfortable with the level of detail in this book, as will the court intellectuals who regard any and all references to the duplicity of groups like the Council on Foreign Relations and the Trilateral Commission as the talk of paranoids completely divorced from reality. Furthermore, people who think that the elimination of corporate influence from the public sphere will finally end the wars and graft will be encouraged to rethink their assumptions about the state: it is not, after all, an organization for the public good that has been hijacked by the rich and powerful, nor an engine of corporate control that can be reformed toward liberal ends. The state itself is and always will be the problem, and so long as it has a military arm, it will be influenced by some private interests or others toward opportunistic warring, and at a minimum manipulated by politicians, even the most supposedly humanitarian and egalitarian of whom have a murderous and diabolical record in deploying its forces and dropping its bombs. Even large business interests can come and go, but the political apparatus itself, the most inherently corrupting of all institutions given its unavoidably coercive and monopolistic nature, will continue to inflict misery and loot the disadvantaged on behalf of the powerful.

On the other hand, unlike moderate libertarians who regard businessmen conspiring with government to be at worst mere accessories to political crime made inevitable by the mixed economy, Rothbard does not temper his indictment of these junior members of the public-private partnerships of imperialist plunder. Free will exists under the Rothbardian conception of both political and economic theory, and if there's blame to go around, the bankers, lobbying CEOs, and saber-rattling policy wonks deserve a considerable share along with the generals and presidents.

In many writings, Rothbard scrutinized the unseemly relations between policymakers and business interests. He championed a revival of libertarian class analysis, reclaiming the exercise from the Marxists and leftists who had transformed it from the study of the tax-consuming political class against the taxpaying subjects into a narrative of the dialectical struggle between producers and workers. Although Marx and his followers correctly attacked the modern state for securing privileges for the most influential business interests, the leftist conception has turned the classical liberal concept of class analysis on its head in its advocacy of proletarian capture of the state apparatus and its casting of producers and entrepreneurs as the inevitable enemies of the common man. Nevertheless, leftist scholars, particularly of the New Left variety, have tended to "follow the money" in their examination of government graft, corruption and war, a task greatly appreciated by Rothbard and his fellow travelers.

In *Wall Street, Banks, and American Foreign Policy*, however, the reader is treated to more nuance and detail as well as a more coherent narrative than are common in the leftist works. This is because the theory behind Rothbard's analysis, unlike the leftist theories, is sound. One general point bears this out. In failing to grasp basic economics, the left falls for the military Keynesianism that often sees war as a blessing for the economy, if not in all other ways. In January 2008, left-liberal economics guru Paul Krugman (who had years earlier called for a Fed-induced housing bubble), complained on his *New York Times* blog:

> One thing I get asked fairly often is whether the Iraq war is responsible for our economic difficulties. The answer (with slight qualifications) is no.... The fact is that war is, in general, *expansionary* for the economy, at least in the short run. World War II, remember, ended the Great Depression.

Even the radicals sometimes mistake neo-mercantilist wars as being in the interest of average American taxpayers—Noam Chomsky has often intoned that the American economy at large relies on these wars—leading to an incomplete critique and a flawed class analysis. This has guided the left in misconstruing George W. Bush's wars for oil as crude attempts to conquer oil fields on behalf of U.S. consumers, rather than as efforts to benefit some firms at the expense of others. (Also largely neglected, compared to the oil angle, were the possible monetary motivations involved, as Iraq had begun pricing its oil in Euros in late 2000, in defiance of American dollar supremacists.) Bad economic theory also meant that when the George H. W. Bush's Secretary of State, James Baker, said the first Gulf War was about "jobs, jobs, jobs," the population was helpless but to take it at face value.

Flawed economic comprehension coincides with a poor reading of history. The left is still largely proud of its heritage in the Progressive Era, when supposedly altruistic politicians stood up for the common man against Big Business. Rothbard unravels this fraud completely. The revered Teddy Roosevelt "had been a Morgan man from the beginning," with family, business and political ties to the banking giant. Roosevelt's "first act after the election of 1900 was to throw a lavish dinner in honor of J.P. Morgan," and many of his policies, from the 1903 Panama coup to the trust busting of Standard Oil, were huge blessings for Morgan interests. The 1912 Progressive Bull Moose Party, far from being an attempt to challenge the pro-business Taft administration for reasons of egalitarian idealism, was also a Morgan plot. The winner of the 1912 election, Woodrow Wilson, far from attempting to rein in the banks via the Federal Reserve Act, was a great champion of the wealthiest of banking elites, especially the Morgans. The Fed itself "enabled the banking system to inflate money and credit, finance loans to the Allies, and float massive deficits once the U.S. entered the war."

More recently, the left-liberal criticisms of Bush suggested that he had broken with an honorable American past in the way he waged war—and in particular condemned his economic motivations as though they were something new or uniquely Republican. Very few critics saw Bush as following a tradition that goes back at least to Franklin Roosevelt's entry into World War II—a war, Rothbard reminds us, the banking elites were pressing for throughout the late 1930s. That war is still sanctified as a testament to human altruism and a struggle of good against evil. But World War II might also "be considered, from one point of view, as a coalition war: the Morgans got *their* war in Europe, the Rockefellers *theirs* in Asia." Henry Stimson, the War Secretary, had been a Wall Street lawyer with as many corporate ties as any modern warmonger, and his assistant John J. McCloy, whom Rothbard exposes for the particularly horrific policy decision of Japanese Internment, went on to a lucrative career in the Rockefeller orbit with a side gig as chairman of the CFR for 17 years. If the military-industrial complex did not exist beforehand, it was a reality by the end of World War II. The *ménage à trois* among the arms merchants, the U.S. war machine, and New York's financial powerhouses became fully consummated even before George W. Bush was born.

Beloved liberal presidents Truman, Kennedy, Johnson and Carter all saturated their defense leadership posts with banking elites. In particular, Rothbard shows that beginning with the Kennedy administration an unsettling influence on foreign policy was enjoyed by representatives from Lehman Brothers and Goldman Sachs—firms whose nefarious impact is not lost on Americans reading the financial news today. The cozy connection between Lehman Brothers and the Pentagon was an especially "fascinating aspect of the Johnson administration." Lehman and other major finance houses also dominated Carter's top brass. Somehow, the left generally regards these presidents as, at worst, pushovers for corporate influence, rather than criminals guilty of premeditated looting and warring on behalf of their cronies.

The financial collapse and bailouts are only the latest example of the near incoherence of the liberal critique. We are to believe that the CEOs of major financial institutions are devoid of compassion, the regulators are neglected heroes mysteriously deprived of power since the Reagan years (although exactly how this was done is never compellingly explained), and the president is at worst a well-intentioned dupe. This formulation is partisan, but even the anti-corporate criticism of Bush betrays a strange faith in government itself, as it accused Bush of failing to "do enough" and insisting on retrenching his own executive branch's power over the economy. All this even after Sarbanes-Oxley and Bush's other major expansions of the regulatory state, far beyond what happened under Bill Clinton.

Today's wars, too, seem to confound the left-liberal who sees corporate interests and conservative agitation behind all policy failures. The war in Iraq, we were told, was a break with American traditions of diplomatic prudence. It is true that the neo-conservatives represented an ideological school unusually bent on democratization by force—hyper-Wilsonians, almost—who indeed signified a shift from the "realist" school that had been economically oriented around the Rockefellers that bestrode policy at least since World War II. For what it's worth, much of the economic establishment was conspicuously more wary of the Iraq war than most U.S. military adventures. This seems something of an anomaly but there was a parallel situation in 1968, when, as Rothbard tells it, even many of the "elite figures" of the Johnson administration "had swung around to a firm opposition to the war," joined by much of the Establishment and Wall Street.

We can only dream of how Rothbard would have reacted to the temporary triumph of the neocons over the realists in Iraq. But needless to say, the general trajectory of U.S. foreign policy—presidential wars of aggression, neo-mercantilism, Fed-financed bombings, trade sanctions, exploiting the UN and NATO when expedient—has been fairly consistent from the Progressive Era to Obama, Bush's aberration notwithstanding. And now the U.S. is solidly back in the "realist" tradition with Obama, who is using international coalitions to obscure the aggression against Libya, and who is continuing the imperial project in Afghanistan that originated with the meddling of Carter's National Security Adviser, Zbigniew Brzezinski, a practical paragon of the realist school. More than a decade after Rothbard wrote this book, identifying Brzezinski as a Trilateral executive director and "recently selected director of the CFR," this establishment poster boy claimed credit for intentionally baiting the Soviets into invading Afghanistan—a fateful intervention that has changed U.S. policy in the Muslim world irreversibly.

When the left attacked the neocons over Iraq—echoing, whether they knew it or not, critiques of neoconservatism that can be traced to Rothbard and his Old-Right tradition—they did not really understand what they were attacking. They neglected almost completely the leftwing and particularly Trotskyite origins of neoconservatism, and tended to downplay the centrality of Israel. They somehow conflated a condemnation of Bush's "privatization" of war, his reliance on military contractors, and his alleged desire to seize Arab oil, with their critique of neoconservatism, even though economics and corporate cronyism were never major interests of this foreign-policy school.

This helps to explain the current confusion, for Obama has greatly increased the presence of military contractors, expanded the war in Afghanistan, bombed Pakistan, Yemen, Somalia, and Libya, and seems generally on board with almost all of the Bush program, including the withdrawal schedule in Iraq. Oil politics and the planned construction of pipelines through Afghanistan are still in the background. The economic and imperial interests behind America's response to 9/11 go far beyond the neocons and their diversion in Iraq.

Of course, the war leaders of the supposedly anomalous Bush years had been establishment luminaries for decades. National Security Adviser and Secretary of State Condolezza Rice was on the first Bush's National Security Council and later served on the board of Chevron. Vice President Dick Cheney (along with Defense Secretary Donald Rumsfeld) had begun his rise under Nixon. Cheney was a director of the Council on Foreign Relations in the late 1980s and, infamously, served in the late 1990s as CEO and Chairman of the Board of Haliburton—the oil services firm that was awarded significant contracts under Clinton during his interventions in the Balkans, became a major beneficiary of Bush's war in Iraq (as well as constructing holding cells for the prison camp at Guantánamo Bay), and still maintains such ties to the empire.

Cheney, it might be noted, was also a member of the Trilateral Commission—that elite club founded by David Rockefeller that came to dominate the halls of power beginning in the Carter administration. Writing in 1984, Rothbard concludes that regardless of the next election we could expect this organization to be well represented. In addition to Cheney, Trilateral members who have risen or remained high in American government since 1984 include Fed Chairman Alan Greenspan, George H. W. Bush, his national security adviser Brent Scowcroft, Bill and Hillary Clinton, and Clinton cabinet members Lloyd Bentsen (Treasury), Warren Christopher (State Department) and William Cohen (Defense). Fewer Trilateral members have appeared more recently, although aside from Vice President Cheney they include George W. Bush's Treasury Secretary, Paul O'Neill, Obama's economic adviser, Paul Volker, and his foreign policy adviser and ambassador to the United Nations, Susan Rice.

The corporate state's continuities transcend partisanship. Ben Bernanke, Bush's economic adviser and later choice for Fed Chairman, was reappointed to this high seat by Obama. Another holdover from the Bush years is Bush's second Defense Secretary, Robert Gates, whose checkered past includes urging Reagan to sell weapons to Iran in 1985, heading the CIA under George H. W. Bush, and serving on boards for such giants as Fidelity Investments, NACCO Industries and Brinker International.

When Obama chose as Treasury Secretary the young Timothy Geithner the man was already a precocious fixture of the establishment. He worked for Kissinger Associates in DC and then joined the U.S. Treasury Department's International Affairs division in 1988. He went on to work for the U.S. embassy in Tokyo, served as an assistant in monetary and financial policy for years, always with an international focus, and became Under Secretary of the Treasury for International Affairs in 1998. In 2002, he was a Senior Fellow in the International Economics department at the Council on Foreign Relations, while also serving as director of the Policy Development and Review Department at the International Monetary Fund. In late 2003, he became the president of the Federal Reserve Bank of New York and then the Vice Chairman of the Federal Open Market Committee. In March 2008 he was intimately involved in the bailout and sale of Bear Stearns. In the wake of the financial meltdown, Obama's choice of Geithner to head Treasury was surreally touted far and wide as a pragmatic, responsible move. But even the minor appointments demonstrate the irony of Obama's reputation as a champion of the common man against Big Business—the president's pick of General Electric CEO Jeffrey Immelt to oversee the effort to curb unemployment rhymes nicely with FDR's pick of GE CEO Gerard Swope to head the National Recovery Administration.

Of course, Obama himself is deeply in the pocket of the finance industry. Goldman Sachs accounted for over $994,000 of Obama's war chest. Lehman Brothers was the origin of $395,600, a record amount for the company second only to what Hillary Clinton received. Out of 20 of his biggest sources of campaign money, eleven were investment banks or closely associated law firms. Justin Raimondo noted in 2008 that Obama's fat cat donors included top executives from Wachovia, Washington Mutual, Citigroup, Deutsche Bank, Merrill Lynch, Bank of America, J. P. Morgan, Chase, Morgan Stanley and Countrywide.

Recent events demonstrate the pervasive denial of the banking and foreign policy nexus. In February 2010, Congressman Ron Paul caused a stir in the House of Representatives when, confronting Bernanke, he noted that "it has been reported in the past that during the 1980s the Fed actually facilitated a $5.5 billion dollar loan to Saddam Hussein, and then he bought weapons from our military industrial complex." Bernanke found the allegation too absurd to warrant a serious response. Paul later cited University of Texas professor Robert D. Auerbach, author of the 2008 book *Deception and Abuse at the Fed* and professor at University of Texas, to defend his statement. Whether or not Bernanke was sincere in his disbelief of this nefarious connection between the Fed and U.S. diplomacy, many onlookers were similarly incredulous.

In March 2011, as the Obama administration was bombing Libya, Senator Bernie Sanders wrote an open letter to Bernanke, asking why the Fed provided 45 emergency loans at nearly zero interest, totaling over $26 billion, to the central bank of Libya from December 2007 to March 2010. He further asked why the bank and its two New York branches were exempted from U.S. sanctions on Libyan businesses.

Meanwhile, the media celebrated the supposed success of TARP, the $700 billion bailout package passed at the tail end of the George W. Bush presidency. At that time we had been told it was necessary or else the financial collapse would swallow the economy whole. Most Americans were skeptical, suspecting they were being robbed by the very forces responsible for the crisis in the first place. The AP reported on March 30, 2011, amidst the official vindication of TARP: "Some banks will use money from a government program aimed at increasing small business loans to repay their federal bailouts, according to the Treasury Department official who oversees the bailout program." The headline was more concise: "Banks will use Fed funds to repay Fed bailout."

Since the publication of *Wall Street, Banks, and American Foreign Policy* a number of other works have emerged in the Rothbardian tradition of tracing the history of the central banking elite and its warfare state conspirators. G. Edward Griffin's extensive book *The Creature from Jekyll Island* (1994), addressing economic theory and history predating the material covered here by Rothbard, is particularly worth mentioning. Robert Higgs's 2007 book *Depression War and Cold War* examines the defense industry's role in World War II and the Cold War. For the definitive treatment on World War I corporatism, with an emphasis on arms merchants as well as the banks, see T. Hunt Tooley's "*Merchants of Death* Revisited: Armaments, Bankers, and the First World War," from the Winter 2004 edition of the *Journal of Libertarian Studies*. It includes a bibliography of many great references.

As for the issues of the 21st century, there are not many survey works on the connections between the war machine and the banking establishment. John Perkins's *Confessions of an Economic Hitman* (2004) tells his story as an agent of international finance with ties to the U.S. security state, convincing Third World nations to accept crushing loans. William D. Hartung's *How Much Are You Making on the War Daddy? A Quick and Dirty Guide to War Profiteering in the Bush Administration* (2003) and Nick Turse's *The Complex: How the Military Invades Our Everyday Lives* (2008) are decent treatments on military corporatism. On the financial collapse and frauds, the investigative journalism of Matt Taibbi, who writes in *Rolling Stone* with a focus on Goldman Sachs, has culminated in his 2010 book *Griftopia: Bubble Machines, Vampire*

Squids, and the Long Con That Is Breaking America. Finally, one article in the *Huffington Post* deserves mention for daring to show the relationship between the central bank and America's court intellectuals: Ryan Grim's "Priceless: How The Federal Reserve Bought The Economics Profession," which appeared in October 2009.

What's missing from most accounts of 21st century war and banking, however, is a sound, Austro-libertarian class analysis combined with a grasp of the business cycle, the meaning of human action in the military-industrial complex, and the inherently predatory nature of the state. Joe Salerno's 2006 work, "Praxeology and the Logic of Warmaking," helps to set the theoretical grounding that war, like all purposeful human activities, has an economic logic to it and can be understood in terms of what its perpetrators seek to gain. For an Austrian treatment of the housing crisis and the corruption in defense spending, Tom Woods's 2011 book *Rollback: Repealing Big Government Before the Coming Fiscal Collapse* provides some helpful chapters. Ron Paul's *End the Fed* has a section on inflation and war. Plenty of articles on different facets of the imperial corporate state can be found on Mises.org, LewRockwell.com, Antiwar.com and elsewhere.

But it would be great to see something like a sequel to *Wall Street, Banks, and American Foreign Policy*, a comprehensive and detailed but concise history starting where Rothbard left off during the Reagan administration and bringing us up to date for today. Until then, we can be satisfied to read this wondrous work of revisionist economic history, class analysis and antiwar journalism all packed into one. To understand modern America, the banking masters and warmongers who've run the show for well over a century must be exposed. To this day, no one has done it as well as Rothbard.

Introduction to the 1995 Edition

By Justin Raimondo

Murray Rothbard's 1984 analysis of modern American history as a great power struggle between economic elites, between the House of Morgan and the Rockefeller interests, culminates in the following conclusion: "The financial power elite can sleep well at night regardless of who wins in 1984." By the time you get there, the conclusion seems understated indeed, for what we have here is a sweeping and compressed history of twentieth century politics from a power elite point of view. It represents a small and highly specialized sample of Rothbard's vast historical knowledge coming together with a lifetime devoted to methodological individualism in the social sciences. It appeared first in 1984, in the thick of the Reagan years, in a small financial publication called *World Market Perspective*. It was printed for a larger audience by the Center for Libertarian Studies in 1995, and appeared online for the first time in 2005.

Theoreticians Left and Right are constantly referring to abstract "forces" when they examine and attempt to explain historical patterns. Applying the principle of methodological individualism—which attributes all human action to individual *actors*—and the economic principles of the Austrian School, Rothbard formulated a trenchant overview of the American elite and the history of the modern era.

Rothbard's analysis flows, first, from the basic principles of Austrian economics, particularly the Misesian analysis of banking and the origin of the business cycle. This issue is also discussed and elaborated on in one of his last books, *The Case Against the Fed* (Mises Institute, 1995). Here, the author relates the history of how the Federal Reserve System came to be foisted on the unsuspecting American people by a high-powered alliance of banking interests. Rothbard's economic analysis is clear, concise, and wide-ranging, covering the nature of money, the genesis of government paper money, the inherent instability (and essential fraudulence) of fractional reserve banking, and the true causes of the business cycle.

As Rothbard explains in his economic writings, the key is in understanding that money is a commodity, like any other, and thus subject to the laws of the market. A government-granted monopoly in this, the very lifeblood of the economic system, is a recipe for inflation, a debased currency—and the creation of a permanent plutocracy whose power is virtually unlimited.

In the present essay, as in *The Case Against the Fed*, it is in the section on the history of the movement to establish the Federal Reserve System that the Rothbardian power elite analysis comes into full and fascinating play. What is striking about this piece is the plethora of details. Rothbard's argument is so jam-packed with facts detailing the social, economic, and familial connections of the burgeoning Money Power, that we need to step back and look at it in the light of Rothbardian theory, specifically Rothbard's theory of class analysis.

Rothbard eagerly reclaimed the concept of class analysis from the Marxists, who expropriated it from the French theorists of *laissez-faire*. Marx authored a plagiarized, distorted, and vulgarized version of the theory based on the Ricardian labor theory of value. Given this premise, he came up with a class analysis pitting workers against owners.

One of Rothbard's many great contributions to the cause of liberty was to restore the original theory, which pitted the people against the State. In the Rothbardian theory of class struggle, the government, including its clients and enforcers, exploits and enslaves the productive classes through taxation, regulation, and perpetual war. Government is an incubus, a parasite, incapable of producing anything in its own right, and instead feeds off the vital energies and productive ability of the producers.

This is the first step of a fully-developed libertarian class analysis. Unfortunately, this is where the thought processes of all too many alleged libertarians come to a grinding halt. It is enough, for them, to know the State is the Enemy, as if it were an irreducible primary.

As William Pitt put it in 1770, "There is something behind the throne greater than the king himself." Blind to the real forces at work on account of their methodological error, Left-libertarians are content to live in a world of science fiction and utopian schemes, in which they are no threat to the powers that be, and are thus tolerated and at times even encouraged.

The Left-libertarian failure to take the analytical process one step further is, in many cases, a failure of nerve. For it is clear, given libertarian theory and the economic insights of the Austrian School, where the next step leads. No empirical evidence is necessary, at this point (although that will come later, and in spades); the truth can be deduced from pure theory, specifically the Austrian theory of the nature of money and banking, and the Misesian analysis of the origin of the business cycle.

This deduction was brilliantly and colorfully made in the first issue of *The Journal of Libertarian Studies* (Winter 1977), by two students of Rothbard, Walter E. Grinder and John Hagel III, in "Toward a Theory of State Capitalism: Ultimate Decision-Making and Class Structure."

While a pure free market would necessarily prevent the development of a banking monopoly, "the market system does concentrate entrepreneurial activity and decision-making within the capital market because of the considerable benefits which are rendered by a certain degree of specialization."

This "specialized capital market, by the very nature of its integrative role within the market system, will emerge as a strategic locus of ultimate decision-making." Given that some individuals will choose the political means over the economic, some of these great fortunes will utilize their tremendous resources to cartelize the market and insulate themselves against risk. The temptation for bankers in particular to wield the power of the State to their benefit is very great because it permits banks to inflate their asset base systematically. The creation of assets made possible by these measures to a great extent frees the banking institutions from the constraints imposed by the passive form of ultimate decision-making exercised by their depositors. It thereby considerably strengthens the ultimate decision-making authority held by banks *vis-à-vis* their depositors. The inflationary trends resulting from the creation of assets tend to increase the ratio of external financing to internal financing in large corporations and, as a consequence, the ultimate decision-making power of banking institutions increases over the activities of industrial corporations.

The Austrian insight focuses on the key role played by the central banks in generating the distortion of market signals that leads to periodic booms and busts, the dreaded business cycle which is always blamed on the inherent contradictions of unfettered capitalism.

But in fact this capitalism is anything but unfettered. (Try starting your own private bank!) The last thing American bankers want is an unfettered banking system. Rothbard not only traces the original market distortion that gives rise to the business cycle, but also identifies the source (and chief beneficiaries) of this distortion. It was Mises who pointed out that government intervention in the economy invariably leads to yet more intervention in order to "fix" the havoc wreaked—and there is a certain logic in the fact that it was the original culprits who decided to "fix" the distortions and disruptions caused by their policies with further assaults on the market mechanism. As Grinder and Hagel put it:

In the U.S., this intervention initially involved sporadic measures, both at the federal and state level, which generated inflationary distortion in the monetary supply and cyclical disruptions of economic activity. The disruptions which accompanied the business cycle were a major factor in the transformation of the dominant ideology in the U.S. from a general adherence to laissez-faire doctrines to an ideology of political capitalism which viewed the state as a necessary instrument for the rationalization and stabilization of an inherently unstable economic order.

CAPITALISTS AS ENEMIES OF CAPITALISM

This explains the strange historical fact, recounted at length and in detail by Rothbard, that the biggest capitalists have been the deadliest enemies of true capitalism. For virtually all of the alleged social "reforms" of the past fifty years were pushed not only by "idealistic" Leftists, but by the very corporate combines caricatured as the top-hatted, pot-bellied "economic royalists" of Wall Street.

The neoconservative Right depicts the battle against Big Government as a two-sided Manichean struggle between the forces of light (that is, of capitalism) and the remnants of largely discredited Leftist elites. But Rothbard's historical analysis reveals a much richer, more complex pattern: instead of being two-sided, the struggle for liberty pits at least three sides against each other. For the capitalists, as John T. Flynn, Albert Jay Nock, and Frank Chodorov all pointed out, were never for capitalism. As Nock put it:

> It is one of the few amusing things in our rather stodgy world that those who today are behaving most tremendously about collectivism and the Red menace are the very ones who have cajoled, bribed, flattered and bedeviled the State into taking each and every one of the successive steps that lead straight to collectivism. ["Impostor Terms," *Atlantic Monthly*, February 1936.]

The New Deal economic policy was, as Rothbard demonstrated, prefigured by Herbert Hoover, champion of big business, and foreshadowed in the reforms of the Progressive era. As the revisionist economic historians, such as Gabriel Kolko, have shown, those who regulated the great industries in the name of progressive "reform" were recruited from the very cartels and trusts they were created to tame.

And of course the monopolists didn't mind being tamed, so long as their competitors were tamed (if not eliminated). Every giant leap forward of economic planning and centralization—central banking, the welfare state, "civil rights," and affirmative action—was supported if not initiated by the biggest and most politically powerful business interests in the country. The House of Morgan, the Rockefellers, and the Kuhn-Loebs must take their place alongside the First, Second, and Third Internationals as the historic enemies of liberty.

Giant multinational corporations, and their economic satellites, in alliance with governments and the big banks, are in the process of extending their influence on a global scale: they dream of a world central bank, global planning, and an international welfare state, with American troops policing the world to guarantee their profit margins.

After the long battle to create a central bank in the U.S., the high priests of high finance finally seized and consolidated control of domestic economic policy. It only remained for them to extend their dominance internationally, and for this purpose they created the Council on Foreign Relations, and, later, the Trilateral Commission.

These two groups have been seized upon by the new populist Right as the virtual embodiments of the Power Elite, and rightly so. It is only by reading Rothbard, however, that this insight is placed in its proper historical perspective. For the fact of the matter is that, as Rothbard shows, the CFR/Trilateralist network is merely the latest incarnation of a trend deeply rooted in modern American history. Long before the founding of the CFR or the Trilateral Commission, there was a power elite in this country; that elite will likely endure long after those organizations are gone or transmuted into something else. Rothbard's unmasking of the historical and economic roots of this trend is vital in understanding that this is not a "conspiracy" centered in the CFR and the Trilateralist groups, as such, but an ideological trend traditionally centered in the Northeast, among the upper classes, and deeply rooted in American history.

I put the word "conspiracy" in quotes because it has become the favorite swearword of the Respectable Right and the "extremist"-baiting Left. If it is conspiracy-mongering to believe that human beings engage in purposeful activity to achieve their economic, political, and personal goals, then rational men and women must necessarily plead guilty. The alternative is to assert that human action is purposeless, random, and inexplicable. History, in this view, is a series of discontinuous accidents.

Yet it would be inaccurate to call the Rothbardian world view a "conspiracy theory." To say that the House of Morgan was engaged in a "conspiracy" to drag the U.S. into World War I, when indeed it *openly* used every stratagem, every lever both economic and political, to push us into "the war to end all wars," seems woefully inadequate. This was not some secret cabal meeting in a soundproof corporate boardroom, but a "conspiracy" of ideas openly and vociferously expressed. (On this point, please note and underscore Rothbard's analysis of the founding of *The New Republic* as the literary flagship of "the growing alliance for war and statism" between the Morgan interests and liberal intellectuals—and isn't it funny how some things never change?)

A conspiracy theory attributes virtually all social problems to a single monolithic agency. Radical feminism, which attributes all the evil in the world to the existence of men, is a classic conspiracy theory; the paranoid views of the ex-Communists in the conservative movement, who were obsessed with destroying their ex-comrades, was another.

But the complexity and subtlety of the Rothbardian analysis, backed up by the sheer mass of rich historical detail, sets Rothbard on an altogether different and higher plane. Here there is no single agency, no omnipotent central committee that issues directives, but a multiplicity of interest groups and factions whose goals are generally congruent.

In this milieu, there are familial, social, and economic connections, as well as ideological complicity, and none is better than Rothbard at ferreting out and unraveling these biographical details. Taken together, the author's small and studied brushstrokes paint a portrait of a ruling class whose ruthlessness is surpassed only by its brazen disloyalty to the nation.

It is a portrait that remains unchanged, in its essentials, to this day. *Wall Street, Banks, and American Foreign Policy* was written and published in 1984, during the Reagan years.

Reagan started out by denouncing the power elite and specifically the CFR and the Trilateralists, but wound up with that epitome of the Establishment, Skull-&-Bonesman George Bush as his vice president and successor.

Bush is a longtime CFR director, and Trilateralist; most of his major cabinet officers, including his chairman of the joint chiefs, Colin Powell, were CFR members. The Clinton administration is similarly afflicted, from the President (CFR/Trilateral) on down through Donna Shalala (CFR/Trilateral) and George Stephanopoulos (CFR), with the CFR honeycombed (as usual) throughout the State Department. In addition to Secretary of State Warren Christopher, other CFR members in the Clinton cabinet include Laura Tyson, chairman of the Council of Economic Advisors, Treasury Secretary Robert Rubin; Interior Secretary Bruce Babbitt, HUD honcho Henry Cisneros; and Alice Rivlin, OMB director.

The other side of the aisle is equally co-opted at the leadership level, as vividly dramatized by Gingrich's retreat before the power and majesty of Henry Kissinger. One naturally expects cowardice from politicians, but the indictment also includes what passes for the intellectual leaders of the Republican free-market "revolution."

There is a certain mentality that, no matter how convincing the evidence, would never even consider the argument put forward in *Wall Street, Banks, and American Foreign Policy.* This attitude stems from a particular kind of cowardice. It is a fear, first of all, of not being listened to, a dread of consigning oneself to the role of Cassandra, the ancient Greek prophetess who was granted the power of foresight by the gods, with but a single limitation: that none would ever heed her warnings. It is far easier, and so much more lucrative, to play the role of court historian.

This is a role the author of this scintillating pamphlet never could have played, even if he had tried. For the truth (or, at least, the search for it) is so much more interesting than the official histories and the conventional wisdom of the moment. The sheer pleasure Rothbard took in unearthing the truth, in carrying out his vocation as a true scholar, is evident not only on every page of the present work but throughout his 28 books and thousands of articles and speeches.

Rothbard was not afraid of sharing Cassandra's fate because, in the first place, truth is a value in its own right, and ought to be upheld for its own sake. Second, the truth has a way of eventually getting out, in spite of the most strenuous efforts to suppress it.

WALL STREET, BANKS, AND AMERICAN FOREIGN POLICY

BUSINESSMEN OR MANUFACTURERS can either be genuine free enterprisers or statists; they can either make their way on the free market or seek special government favors and privileges. They choose according to their individual preferences and values. But bankers are inherently inclined toward statism.

Commercial bankers, engaged as they are in unsound fractional reserve credit, are, in the free market, always teetering on the edge of bankruptcy. Hence they are always reaching for government aid and bailout.

Investment bankers do much of their business underwriting government bonds, in the United States and abroad. Therefore, they have a vested interest in promoting deficits and in forcing taxpayers to redeem government debt. Both sets of bankers, then, tend to be tied in with government policy, and try to influence and control government actions in domestic and foreign affairs.

In the early years of the nineteenth century, the organized capital market in the United States was largely confined to government bonds (then called "stocks"), along with canal companies and banks themselves. Whatever investment banking existed was therefore concentrated in government debt. From the Civil War until the 1890s, there were virtually no manufacturing corporations; manufacturing and other businesses were partnerships and had not yet reached the size where they needed to adopt the corporate form. The only exception was railroads, the biggest industry in the U.S. The first investment banks, therefore, were concentrated in railroad securities and government bonds.

The first major investment banking house in the United States was a creature of government privilege. Jay Cooke, an Ohio-born business promoter living in Philadelphia, and his brother Henry, editor of the leading Republican newspaper in Ohio, were close friends of Ohio U.S. Senator Salmon P. Chase. When the new Lincoln administration took over in 1861, the Cookes lobbied hard to secure Chase the appointment of Secretary of the Treasury. That lobbying, plus the then-enormous sum of $100,000 that Jay Cooke poured into Chase's political coffers, induced Chase to return the favor by granting Cooke, newly set up as an investment banker, an enormously lucrative monopoly in underwriting the entire federal debt.

Cooke and Chase then managed to use the virtual Republican monopoly in Congress during the war to transform the American commercial banking system from a relatively free market to a National Banking System centralized by the federal government under Wall Street control. A crucial aspect of that system was that national banks could only expand credit in proportion to the federal bonds they owned—bonds which they were forced to buy from Jay Cooke.

Jay Cooke & Co. proved enormously influential in the postwar Republican administrations, which continued their monopoly in underwriting government bonds. The House of Cooke met its well-deserved fate by going bankrupt in the Panic of 1874, a failure helped along by its great rival, the then Philadelphia-based Drexel, Morgan & Co.

J. P. Morgan

After 1873, Drexel, Morgan and its dominant figure, J. P. Morgan, became by far the leading investment firm in the U.S. If Cooke had been a "Republican" bank, Morgan, while prudently well connected in both parties, was chiefly influential among the Democrats. The other great financial interest powerful in the Democratic Party was the mighty European investment banking house of the Rothschilds, whose agent, August Belmont, was treasurer of the national Democratic party for many years.

The enormous influence of the Morgans on the Democratic administrations of Grover Cleveland (1885–89, 1893–97), may be seen by simply glancing at their leading personnel. Grover Cleveland himself spent virtually all his life in the Morgan ambit. He grew up in Buffalo as a railroad lawyer, one of his major clients being the Morgan-dominated New York Central Railroad. In between administrations, he became a partner of the powerful New York City law firm of Bangs, Stetson, Tracey, and MacVeagh. This firm, by the late 1880s, had become the chief legal firm of the House of Morgan, largely because senior partner Charles B. Tracey was J. P. Morgan's brother-in-law. After Tracey died in 1887, Francis Lynde Stetson, an old and close friend of Cleveland's, became the firm's dominant partner, as well as the personal attorney for J. P. Morgan. (This is now the Wall St. firm of Davis, Polk, and Wardwell.)

Grover Cleveland's cabinets were honeycombed with Morgan men, with an occasional bow to other bankers. Considering those officials most concerned with foreign policy, his first Secretary of State, Thomas F. Bayard, was a close ally and disciple of August Belmont; indeed, Belmont's son, Perry, had lived with and worked for Bayard in Congress as his top aide. The dominant Secretary of State in the second Cleveland administration was the powerful Richard Olney, a leading lawyer for Boston financial interests, who have always been tied in with the Morgans, and in particular was on the Board of the Morgan-run Boston and Maine Railroad, and would later help Morgan organize the General Electric Company.

The War and Navy departments under Cleveland were equally banker-dominated. Boston Brahmin Secretary of War William C. Endicott had married into the wealthy Peabody family. Endicott's wife's uncle, George Peabody, had established a banking firm which included J. P. Morgan's father as a senior partner; and a Peabody had been best man at J.P.'s wedding. Secretary of the Navy was leading New York City financier William C. Whitney, a close friend and top political advisor of Cleveland's. Whitney was closely allied with the Morgans in running the New York Central Railroad.

Secretary of War in the second Cleveland administration was an old friend and aide of Cleveland's, Daniel S. Lamont, previously an employee and protégé of William C. Whitney. Finally, the second Secretary of the Navy was an Alabama Congressman, Hilary A. Herbert, an attorney for and very close friend of Mayer Lehman, a founding partner of the New York mercantile firm of Lehman Brothers, soon to move heavily into investment banking. Indeed, Mayer's son, Herbert, later to be Governor of New York during the New Deal, was named after Hilary Herbert.

The great turning point of American foreign policy came in the early 1890s, during the second Cleveland administration. It was then that the U.S. turned sharply and permanently from a foreign policy of peace and non-intervention to an aggressive program of economic and political expansion abroad. At the heart of the new policy were America's leading bankers, eager to use the country's growing economic strength to subsidize and force-feed export markets and investment outlets that they would finance, as well as to guarantee Third World government bonds. The major focus of aggressive expansion in the 1890s was Latin America, and the principal Enemy to be dislodged was Great Britain, which had dominated foreign investments in that vast region.

In a notable series of articles in 1894, *Bankers' Magazine* set the agenda for the remainder of the decade. Its conclusion: if "we could wrest the South American markets from Germany and England and permanently hold them, this would be indeed a conquest worth perhaps a heavy sacrifice."

Longtime Morgan associate Richard Olney heeded the call, as Secretary of State from 1895 to 1897, setting the U.S. on the road to Empire. After leaving the State Department, he publicly summarized the policy he had pursued. The old isolationism heralded by George Washington's Farewell Address is over, he thundered. The time has now arrived, Olney declared, when "it behooves us to accept the commanding position ... among the Power of the earth." And, "the present crying need of our commercial interests," he added, "is more markets and larger markets" for American products, especially in Latin America.

Good as their word, Cleveland and Olney proceeded belligerently to use U.S. might to push Great Britain out of its markets and footholds in Latin America. In 1894, the United States Navy illegally used force to break the blockade of Rio de Janeiro by a British-backed rebellion aiming to restore the Brazilian monarchy. To insure that the rebellion was broken, the U.S. Navy stationed warships in Rio harbor for several months.

During the same period, the U.S. government faced a complicated situation in Nicaragua, where it was planning to guarantee the bonds of the American Maritime Canal Company to build a canal across the country. The new regime of General

Zelaya was threatening to revoke this canal concession; at the same time an independent reservation of Mosquito Indians, protected for decades by Great Britain, sat athwart the eastern end of the proposed canal. In a series of deft maneuvers, using the Navy and landing the Marines, the U.S. managed to bring Zelaya to heel and to oust the British and take over the Mosquito territory.

In Santo Domingo (now the Dominican Republic) France was the recipient of the American big stick. In the Santo Domingo Improvement Company, in 1893, a consortium of New York bankers purchased the entire debt of Santo Domingo from a Dutch company, receiving the right to collect all Dominican customs revenues in payment of the debt. The French became edgy the following year when a French citizen was murdered in that country, and the French government threatened to use force to obtain reparations. Its target for reparations was the Dominican customs revenue, at which point the U.S. sent a warship to the area to intimidate the French.

But the most alarming crisis of this period took place in 1895–96, when the U.S. was at a hair's breadth from actual war with Great Britain over a territorial dispute between Venezuela and British Guiana. This boundary dispute had been raging for forty years, but Venezuela shrewdly attracted American interest by granting concessions to Americans in gold fields in the disputed area.

Apparently, Cleveland had had enough of the "British threat," and he moved quickly toward war. His close friend Don Dickinson, head of the Michigan Democratic Party, delivered a bellicose speech in May 1895 as a surrogate for the President. Wars are inevitable, Dickinson declared, for they arise out of commercial competition between nations. The United States faces the danger of numerous conflicts, and clearly the enemy was Great Britain. After reviewing the history of the alleged British threat, Dickinson thundered that "we need and must have open markets throughout the world to maintain and increase our prosperity."

In July, Secretary of State Olney sent the British an insulting and tub-thumping note, declaring that "the United States is practically sovereign on this continent, and its fiat is law upon the subjects to which it confines its interposition." President Cleveland, angry at the British rejection of the note, delivered a virtual war message to Congress in December, but Britain, newly occupied in problems with the Boers in South Africa, decided to yield and agree to a compromise boundary settlement. Insultingly, the Venezuelans received not a single seat on the agreed-upon arbitration commission.

In effect, the British, occupied elsewhere, had ceded dominance to the United States in Latin America. It was time for the U.S. to find more enemies to challenge.

The next, and greatest, Latin American intervention was of course in Cuba, where a Republican administration entered the war goaded by its jingo wing closely allied to the Morgan interests, led by young Assistant Secretary of the Navy Theodore Roosevelt and by his powerful Boston Brahmin mentor, Senator Henry Cabot Lodge. But American intervention in Cuba had begun in the Cleveland-Olney regime.

In February 1895, a rebellion for Cuban independence broke out against Spain. The original U.S. response was to try to end the threat of revolutionary war to American property interests by siding with Spanish rule modified by autonomy to the Cubans to pacify their desires for independence. Here was the harbinger of U.S. foreign policy ever since: to try to maneuver in Third World countries to sponsor "third force" or "moderate" interests which do not really exist. The great proponent of this policy was the millionaire sugar grower in Cuba Edwin F. Atkins, a close friend of fellow-Bostonian Richard Olney and a partner of J. P. Morgan and Company.

By the fall of 1895, Olney concluded that Spain could not win, and that, in view of the "large and important commerce between the two countries" and the "large amounts of American capital" in Cuba, the U.S. should execute a 180-degree shift and back the rebels, even unto recognizing Cuban independence. The fact that such recognition would certainly lead to war with Spain did not seem worth noting. The road to war with Spain had begun, a road that would reach its logical conclusion three years later.

Ardently backing the pro-war course was Edwin F. Atkins, and August Belmont, on behalf of the Rothschild banking interests. The House of Rothschild, which had been long-time financiers to Spain, refused to extend any further credit to Spain, and instead underwrote Cuban Revolutionary bond issues, and even assumed full obligation for the unsubscribed balance.

During the conquest of Cuba in the Spanish-American War, the United States also took the occasion to expand its power greatly in Asia, seizing first the port of Manila and then all of the Philippines, after which it spent several years crushing the revolutionary forces of the Philippine independence movement.

An Aggressive Asian Policy

The late 1890s also saw a new turn in the United States' attitude toward the Far East. Expanding rapidly into the Pacific in pursuit of economic and financial gain, the U.S. government saw that Russia, Germany, and France had been carving up increasing territorial and economic concessions in the near corpse of the Chinese imperial dynasty. Coming late in the imperial game of Asia, and not willing to risk large scale expenditure of troops, the U.S., led by Olney and continued by the Republicans, decided to link up with Great Britain. The two countries would then use the Japanese to provide the shock troops that would roll back Russia and Germany and parcel out imperial benefits to both of her faraway allies, in a division of spoils known euphemistically as the "Open Door." With Britain leaving the field free to the U.S. in Latin America, the U.S. could afford to link arms in friendly fashion with Britain in the Far East.

A major impetus toward a more aggressive policy in Asia was provided by the lure of railroad concessions. Lobbying heavily for railroad concessions was the American China Development Company, organized in 1895 and consisting of a consortium of the top financial interests in the U.S., including James Stillman of the then Rockefeller-controlled National City Bank; Charles Coster, railroad expert of J. P. Morgan and Co.; Jacob Schiff, head of the New York investment bank of Kuhn, Loeb and Co.; and Edward H. Harriman, railroad magnate. Olney and the State Department pressed China hard for concessions to the ACDC for a Peking-Hankow Railway and for a railway across Manchuria, but in both cases the American syndicate was blocked. Russia pressured China successfully to grant that country the right to build a Manchurian railway; and a Belgian syndicate, backed by France and Russia, won the Peking-Hankow concession from China.

It was time for sterner measures. The attorney for the ACDC set up the Committee on American Interests in China, which soon transformed itself into the American Asiatic Association, dedicated to a more aggressive American policy on behalf of economic interests in China. After helping the European powers suppress the nationalist Boxer Rebellion in China in 1900, the U.S. also helped push Russian troops out of Manchuria. Finally, in 1904, President Theodore Roosevelt egged Japan on to attack Russia, and Japan succeeded in driving Russia out of Manchuria and ending Russia's economic concessions. Roosevelt readily acceded to Japan's resulting dominance in Korea and Manchuria, hoping that Japan would also protect American economic interests in the area.

Theodore Roosevelt had been a Morgan man from the beginning of his career. His father and uncle were both Wall Street bankers, both of them closely associated with various Morgan-dominated railroads. Roosevelt's first cousin and major financial adviser, W. Emlen Roosevelt, was on the board of several New York banks, including the Astor National Bank, the president of which was George F. Baker, close friend and ally of J. P. Morgan and head of Morgan's flagship commercial bank, the First National Bank of New York. At Harvard, furthermore, young Theodore married Alice Lee, daughter of George Cabot Lee, and related to the top Boston Brahmin families. Kinsman Henry Cabot Lodge soon became TR's long-time political mentor.

Throughout the nineteenth century, the Republicans had been mainly a high-tariff, inflationist party, while the Democrats had been the party of free trade and hard money, i.e., the gold standard. In 1896, however, the radical inflationist forces headed by

William Jennings Bryan captured the Democratic presidential nomination, and so the Morgans, previously dominant in the Democratic Party, sent a message to the Republican nominee, William McKinley, through Henry Cabot Lodge. Lodge stated that the Morgan interests would back McKinley provided that the Republicans would support the gold standard. The deal was struck.

William McKinley reflected the dominance of the Republican Party by the Rockefeller/Standard Oil interests. Standard Oil was originally headquartered at Rockefeller's home in Cleveland, and the oil magnate had long had a commanding influence in Ohio Republican politics. In the early 1890s, Marcus Hanna, industrialist and high school chum of John D. Rockefeller, banded together with Rockefeller and other financiers to save McKinley from bankruptcy, and Hanna became McKinley's top political adviser and chairman of the Republican National Committee. As a consolation prize to the Morgan interests for McKinley's capture of the Republican nomination, Morgan man Garret A. Hobart, director of various Morgan companies, including the Liberty National Bank of New York City, became Vice-President.

The death of Hobart in 1899 left a "Morgan vacancy" in the Vice-Presidential spot, as McKinley walked into the nomination. McKinley and Hanna were both hostile to Roosevelt, considering him "erratic" and a "Madman," but after several Morgan men turned down the nomination, and after the intensive lobbying of Morgan partner George W. Perkins, Teddy Roosevelt at last received the Vice-Presidential nomination. It is not surprising that virtually Teddy's first act after the election of 1900 was to throw a lavish dinner in honor of J. P. Morgan.

Teddy Roosevelt and the "Lone Nut"

The sudden appearance of one of the "lone nuts" so common in American political history led to the assassination of McKinley, and suddenly Morgan man Theodore Roosevelt was President. John Hay, expansionist Secretary of State whom Roosevelt inherited from McKinley, had the good fortune of having his daughter marry the son of William C. Whitney, of the great Morgan-connected family. TR's next Secretary of State and former Secretary of War was his old friend Elihu Root, personal attorney for J. P. Morgan. Root appointed as his Assistant Secretary a close friend of TR's, Robert Bacon, a Morgan partner, and in due course Bacon became TR's Secretary of State. TR's first appointed Secretary of the Navy was Paul Morton, vice-president of the Morgan-controlled Atchison, Topeka and Santa Fe Railroad, and his Assistant Secretary was Herbert L. Satterlee, who had the distinction of being J. P. Morgan's son-in-law.

Theodore Roosevelt's greatest direct boost to the Morgan interests is little known. It is well-known that Roosevelt engineered a phony revolution in Columbia in 1903, creating the new state of Panama and handing the Canal Zone to the United States. What has not been fully disclosed is who benefited from the $40 million that the U.S. government paid, as part of the Panama settlement, to the owners of the old bankrupt Panama Canal Company, a French company which had previously been granted a Colombian concession to dig a Panama canal.

The Panama Canal Company's lobbyist, Morgan-connected New York attorney William Nelson Cromwell, literally sat in the White House directing the "revolution" and organizing the final settlement. We now know that, in 1900, the shares of the old French Panama Canal Company were purchased by an American financial syndicate, headed by J. P. Morgan & Co., and put together by Morgan's top attorney, Francis Lynde Stetson. The syndicate also included members of the Rockefeller, Seligman, and Kuhn, Loeb financial groups, as well as Perkins and Saterlee.

The syndicate did well from the Panama revolution, purchasing the shares at two-thirds of par and selling them, after the revolution, for double the price. One member of the syndicate was especially fortunate: Teddy Roosevelt's brother-in-law, Douglas E. Robinson, a director of Morgan's Astor National Bank. For William Cromwell was named the fiscal agent of the new Republic of Panama, and Cromwell promptly put $6 million of the $10 million payoff the U.S. made to the Panamanian revolutionaries into New York City mortgages via the real estate firm of the same Douglas E. Robinson.

After the turn of the century, a savage economic and political war developed between the Morgan interests on the one hand, and the allied Harriman-Kuhn, Loeb-Rockefeller interests on the other. Harriman and Kuhn, Loeb grabbed control of the Union Pacific Railroad and the two titanic forces battled to a draw for control of the Northern Pacific. Also, at about the same time, a long-lasting and worldwide financial and political "oil war" broke out between Standard Oil, previously a monopolist in both the crude and export markets outside of the U.S., and the burgeoning British Royal Dutch Shell–Rothschild combine.

And since the Morgans and Rothschilds were longtime allies, it is certainly sensible to conclude—though there are no hard facts to prove it—that Teddy Roosevelt launched his savage anti-trust assault to break Standard Oil as a Morgan contribution to the worldwide struggle. Furthermore, Mellon-owned Gulf Oil was allied to the Shell combine, and this might well explain the fact that former Morgan-and-Mellon lawyer Philander Knox, TR's Attorney-General, was happy to file the suit against Standard Oil.

Roosevelt's successor, William Howard Taft, being an Ohio Republican, was allied to the Rockefeller camp, and so he proceeded to take vengeance on the Morgans by filing anti-trust suits to break up the two leading Morgan trusts, International Harvester and United States Steel. It was now all-out war, and so the Morgans in 1912 deliberately created a new party, the Progressive Party, headed by former Morgan partner, George W. Perkins. The successful aim of the Progressive Party was to bring Theodore Roosevelt out of retirement to run for President, in order to break Taft, and to elect, for the first time in a generation, a Democratic President. The new party was liquidated soon after.

Supporters of Roosevelt were studded with financiers in the Morgan ambit, including Judge Elbert Gary, chairman of the board of U.S. Steel; Medill McCormick of the International Harvester family; and Willard Straight, Morgan's partner. In the same year, Straight and his heiress wife, Dorothy Whitney, founded the weekly magazine of opinion, *The New Republic*, symbolizing the growing alliance for war and statism between the Morgans and various of the more moderate (i.e., non-Marxist) progressive and socialist intellectuals.

Morgan, Wilson, and War

———————

The Morgan-Progressive Party ploy deliberately ensured the election of Woodrow Wilson as a Democratic President. Wilson himself, until almost the time of running for President, was for several years on the board of the Morgan-controlled Mutual Life Insurance Company. He was also surrounded by Morgan men. His son-in-law, William Gibbs McAdoo, who became Wilson's Secretary of the Treasury, was a failing businessman in New York City when he was bailed out and befriended by J. P. Morgan and his associates. The Morgans then set McAdoo up as president of New York's Hudson and Manhattan Railroad until his appointment in the Wilson administration. McAdoo was to spend the rest of his financial and political life securely in the Morgan ambit.

The main sponsor of Wilson's run for the Presidency was George W. Harvey, head of Morgan-controlled Harper & Brothers publishers; other major backers included Wall Street financier and Morgan associate Thomas Fortune Ryan, and Wilson's college classmate and Morgan ally Cyrus H. McCormick, head of International Harvester.

Another close friend and leading political adviser of Wilson was New York City banker George Foster Peabody, son of the Boston Brahmin, and a Morgan banker. A particularly fascinating figure in Wilson's fateful foreign policy was "Colonel" Edward Mandell House, of the wealthy House family of Texas, which was deeply involved in landowning, trade, banking, and railroads. House himself was head for several years of the Trinity and Brazos Valley Railway, financed by the House family in collaboration with Morgan-associated Boston financial interests, particularly of the Old Colony Trust Company. The mysterious House, though never graced with an official government post, is generally acknowledged to have been Wilson's all-powerful foreign policy adviser and aide for virtually his entire two terms.

By 1914, the Morgan empire was in increasingly shaky financial shape. The Morgans had long been committed to railroads, and after the turn of the century the highly subsidized and regulated railroads entered their permanent decline. The Morgans had also not been active enough in the new capital market for industrial securities, which had begun in the 1890s, allowing Kuhn, Loeb to beat them in the race for industrial finance. To make matters worse, the $400 million Morgan-run New Haven Railroad went bankrupt in 1914.

At the moment of great financial danger for the Morgans, the advent of World War I came as a godsend. Long connected to British, including Rothschild, financial interests, the Morgans leaped into the fray, quickly securing the appointment, for J. P. Morgan & Co., of fiscal agent for the warring British and French governments, and monopoly underwriter for their war bonds in the United States. J. P. Morgan also became the fiscal agent for the Bank of England, the powerful English central bank. Not only that: the Morgans were heavily involved in financing American munitions and other firms exporting war material to Britain and France. J. P. Morgan & Co., moreover, became the central authority organizing and channeling war purchases for the two Allied nations.

The United States had been in a sharp recession during 1913 and 1914; unemployment was high, and many factories were operating at only 60% of capacity. In November 1914, Andrew Carnegie, closely allied with the Morgans ever since his Carnegie Steel Corporation had merged into the formation of United States

Steel, wrote to President Wilson lamenting business conditions but happily expecting a great change for the better from Allied purchases of U.S. exports.

Sure enough, war material exports zoomed. Iron and steel exports quintupled from 1914 to 1917, and the average profit rate of iron and steel firms rose from 7.4% to 28.7% from 1915 until 1917. Explosives exports to the Allies rose over ten-fold during 1915 alone. Overall, from 1915 to 1917, the export department of J. P. Morgan and Co. negotiated more than $3 billion of contracts to Britain and France. By early 1915, Secretary McAdoo was writing to Wilson hailing the "great prosperity" being brought by war exports to the Allies, and a prominent business writer wrote the following year that "War, for Europe, is meaning devastation and death; for America a bumper crop of new millionaires and a hectic hastening of prosperity revival."

Deep in Allied bonds and export of munitions, the Morgans were doing extraordinarily well; and their great rivals, Kuhn, Loeb, being pro-German, were necessarily left out of the Allied wartime bonanza. But there was one hitch: it became imperative that the Allies win the war. It is not surprising, therefore, that from the beginning of the great conflict, J. P. Morgan and his associates did everything they possibly could to push the supposedly neutral United States into the war on the side of England and France. As Morgan himself put it: "We agreed that we should do all that was lawfully in our power to help the Allies win the war as soon as possible."

Accordingly, Henry P. Davison, Morgan partner, set up the Aerial Coast Patrol in 1915, to get the public in the mood to search the skies for German planes. Bernard M. Baruch, long-time associate of the extremely wealthy copper magnates, the Guggenheim family, financed the Businessmen's Training Camp, at Plattsburgh, New York, designed to push for universal military training and preparations for war. Also participating in financing the camp were Morgan partner Willard Straight, and former Morgan partner Robert Bacon. In addition to J. P. Morgan himself, a raft of

Morgan-affiliated political leaders whooped it up for immediate entry of the U.S. into the war on the side of the Allies, including Henry Cabot Lodge, Elihu Root, and Theodore Roosevelt.

In addition, the National Security League was founded in December, 1914, to call for American entry into the war against Germany. The NSL issued warnings against a German invasion of the U.S., once England was defeated, and it called all advocates of peace and non-intervention, "pro-German," "dangerous aliens," "traitors," and "spies."

The NSL also advocated universal military training, conscription, and the U.S. buildup of the largest navy in the world. Prominent in the organization of the National Security League were Frederic R. Coudert, Wall Street attorney for the British, French, and Russian governments; Simon and Daniel Guggenheim; T. Coleman DuPont, of the munitions family; and a host of prominent Morgan-oriented financiers, including former Morgan partner Robert Bacon; Henry Clay Frick of Carnegie Steel; Judge Gary of U.S. Steel; George W. Perkins, Morgan partner, who has been termed "the secretary of state" for the Morgan interests; former President Theodore Roosevelt; and J. P. Morgan himself.

A particularly interesting founding associate of NSL was a man who has dominated American foreign policy during the twentieth century: Henry L. Stimson, Secretary of War under William H. Taft and Franklin D. Roosevelt, and Secretary of State under Herbert Hoover. Stimson, a Wall Street lawyer in the Morgan ambit, was a protégé of Morgan's personal attorney, Elihu Root, and two of his cousins were partners in the Morgan-dominated Wall Street utility stock market and banking firm of Bonbright & Co.

While the Morgans and other financial interests were beating the drums for war, even more influential in pushing the only partially reluctant Wilson into the war were his foreign policy Svengali, Colonel House, and House's protégé, Walter Hines Page, who was appointed Ambassador to Great Britain. Page's salary in this prestigious influential post was handsomely subsidized through Colonel House by copper magnate Cleveland H. Dodge, a prominent adviser to Wilson, who benefited greatly from munitions sales to the Allies.

Colonel House liked to pose as an abject instrument of President Wilson's wishes. But before and after U.S. entry into the war House shamelessly manipulated Wilson, in secret and traitorous collaboration with the British, to push the President first into entering the war and then into following British wishes instead of setting an independent American course.

Thus, in 1916, House wrote to his friend Frank L. Polk, Counselor to the State Department and later counselor to J. P. Morgan, that "the President must be guided" not to be independent of British desires. Advising British Prime Minister Arthur Balfour on how best to handle Wilson, House counseled Balfour to exaggerate British difficulties in order to get more American aid, and warned him never to mention a negotiated peace. Furthermore, Balfour leaked to Colonel House the details of various secret Allied treaties that they both knew the naïve Wilson would not accept, and they both agreed to keep the treaties from the President.

Similarly, soon after the U.S. entered the war, the British sent to the U.S., as personal liaison between the Prime Minister and the White House, the young chief of British military intelligence, Sir William Wiseman. House and Wiseman quickly entered a close collaboration, with House coaching the Englishman on the best way of dealing with the President, such as "tell him only what he wants to hear," never argue with him, and discover and exploit his weaknesses.

In turn, Britain's top intelligence agent manipulated House, constantly showering him with flattery, and established a close friendship with the Colonel, getting an apartment in the same building in New York City, and traveling together abroad. Collaborating with House in his plan to manipulate Wilson into pro-British policies was William Phillips, an Assistant Secretary of State who had married into the Astor family.

Collaborating with House in supplying Wiseman with illegal information and working with the British agent against Wilson were two important American officials. One was Walter Lippman, a young socialist who had been named by Morgan partner Willard Straight as one of the three editors of his *New Republic*, a magazine which, needless to say, led the parade of progressive and socialist intellectuals in favor of entering the war on the side of the Allies.

Lippmann soon vaulted into important roles in the war effort: assistant to the Secretary of War, then secretary of the secret group of historians called The Inquiry, established under Colonel House in late 1917 to plan the peace settlement at the end of the war. Lippmann later left The Inquiry to go overseas for American military intelligence.

Another important collaborator with Wiseman was businessman and scholar George Louis Beer, who was in charge of African and Asian colonial matters for The Inquiry. Wiseman secretly showed British documents on African colonies to Beer, who in turn leaked Inquiry reports to British intelligence.

The plans of Colonel House and his biased young historians of The Inquiry were put into effect at the peace settlement at Versailles. Germany, Austria-Hungary, and Russia were cruelly dismembered, thus ensuring that Germany and Russia, once recovered from the devastation of the war, would bend their energies toward getting their territories back. In that way, conditions were virtually set for World War II.

Not only that: the Allies at Versailles took advantage of the temporary power vacuum in Eastern Europe to create new independent states that would function as client states of Britain and France, be part of the Morgan/Rothschild financial network, and help keep Germany and Russia down permanently. It was an impossible task for these new small nations, a task made more difficult by the fact that the young historians managed to rewrite the map of Europe at Versailles to make the Poles, the Czechs, and the Serbs dominant over all the other minority nationalities forcibly incorporated into the new countries. These subjugated peoples—the Germans, Ukrainians, Slovaks, Croats, Slovenes, etc.—thus became built-in allies for the revanchist dreams of Germany and Russia.

American entry into World War I in April 1917 prevented negotiated peace between the warring powers, and drove the Allies forward into a peace of unconditional surrender and dismemberment, a peace which, as we have seen, set the stage for World War II. American entry thus cost countless lives on both sides, caused chaos and disruption throughout central and eastern Europe at war's end, and the consequent rise of Bolshevism, fascism, and Nazism to power in Europe. In this way, Woodrow Wilson's decision to enter the war may have been the single most fateful action of the twentieth century, causing untold and unending misery and destruction. But Morgan profits were expanded and assured.

The Fortuitous Fed

The massive U.S. loans to the Allies, and the subsequent American entry into the war, could not have been financed by the relatively hard-money, gold standard system that existed before 1914. Fortuitously, an institution was established at the end of 1913 that made the loans and war finance possible: the Federal Reserve System. By centralizing reserves, by providing a government-privileged lender of last resort to the banks, the Fed enabled the banking system to inflate money and credit, finance loans to the Allies, and float massive deficits once the U.S. entered the war. In addition, the seemingly odd Fed policy of creating an acceptance market out of thin air by standing ready to purchase acceptance at a subsidized rate, enabled the Fed to rediscount acceptance on munitions exports.

The Federal Reserve was the outgrowth of five years of planning, amending, and compromising among various politicians and concerned financial groups, led by the major financial interests, including the Morgans, the Rockefellers, and the Kuhn, Loebs, along with their assorted economists and technicians.

Particularly notable among the Rockefeller interests were Senator Nelson W. Aldrich (R.–R.I.), father-in-law of John D. Rockefeller, Jr., and Frank A. Vanderlip, vice president of Rockefeller's National City Bank of New York. From the Kuhn, Loebs came the prominent Paul Moritz Warburg, of the German investment banking firm of M. M. Warburg and Company. Warburg emigrated to the United States in 1902 to become a senior partner at Kuhn, Loeb & Co., after which he spent most of his time agitating for a central bank in the United States.

Also igniting the drive for a Federal Reserve System was Jacob H. Schiff, powerful head of Kuhn, Loeb to whom Warburg was related by marriage. Seconding and sponsoring Warburg in academia was the prominent Columbia University economist Edwin R. A. Seligman, of the investment banking family of J. & W. Seligman and Company; Seligman was the brother of Warburg's brother-in-law.

The Morgans were prominently represented in the planning and agitation for a Central Bank by Henry P. Davison, Morgan partner; Charles D. Norton, president of Morgan's First National Bank of New York; A. Barton Hepburn, head of Morgan's Chase National Bank; and Victor Morawetz, attorney and banker in the Morgan ranks and chairman of the executive committee of the Morgan-controlled Atchison, Topeka, and Santa Fe Railroad.

While the establishment of the Federal Reserve System in late 1913 was the result of a coalition of Morgan, Rockefeller, and Kuhn, Loeb interests, there is no question which financial group controlled the personnel and the policies of the Fed once it was established. (While influential in framing policies of the Fed, Federal Reserve Board member Warburg was disqualified from leadership because of his pro-German views.) The first Federal Reserve Board, appointed by President Wilson in 1914, included Warburg; one Rockefeller man, Frederic A. Delano, uncle of Franklin D. Roosevelt, and president of the Rockefeller-controlled Wabash Railway; and an Alabama banker, who had both Morgan and Rockefeller connections.

Overshadowing these three were three definite Morgan men, and a university economist, Professor Adolph C. Miller of Berkeley, whose wife's family had Morgan connections. The three definite Morgan men were Secretary of the Treasury McAdoo; Comptroller of the Currency John Skelton Williams, a Virginia banker and long-time McAdoo aide on Morgan railroads; and

Assistant Secretary of the Treasury Charles S. Hamlin, a Boston attorney who had married into a wealthy Albany family long connected with the Morgan-dominated New York Central Railroad.

But more important than the composition of the Federal Reserve Board was the man who became the first Governor of the New York Federal Reserve Bank and who single-handedly dominated Fed policy from its inception until his death in 1928. This man was Benjamin Strong, who had spent virtually his entire business and personal life in the circle of top associates of J. P. Morgan. A secretary of several trust companies (banks doing trust business) in New York City, Strong became neighbor and close friend of three top Morgan partners, Henry P. Davison, Dwight Morrow, and Thomas W. Lamont. Davison, in particular, became his mentor, and brought him into Morgan's Bankers Trust company, where he soon succeeded Lamont as vice-president, and then finally became president. When Strong was offered the post of Governor of the New York Fed, it was Davison who persuaded him to take the job.

Strong was an enthusiast for American entry into the war, and it was his mentor Davison who had engineered the coup of getting Morgan named as sole underwriter and purchasing agent for Britain and France. Strong worked quickly to formalize collaboration with the Bank of England, collaboration which would continue in force throughout the 1920s. The Federal Reserve Bank of New York became foreign agent for the Bank of England, and vice versa.

The main collaboration throughout the 1920s, much of it kept secret from the Federal Reserve Board in Washington, was between Strong and the man who soon became Governor of the Bank of England, Montagu Collet Norman. Norman and Strong were not only fast friends, but had important investment banking ties, Norman's uncle having been a partner of the great English banking firm of Baring Brothers, and his grandfather a partner in the international banking house of Brown Shipley & Co., the London branch of the Wall Street banking firm of Brown

Brothers. Before coming to the Bank of England, Norman himself had worked at the Wall Street office of Brown Brothers, and then returned to London to become a partner of Brown Shipley.

The major fruit of the Norman-Strong collaboration was Strong's being pressured to inflate money and credit in the U.S. throughout the 1920s, in order to keep England from losing gold to the U.S. from its inflationary policies. Britain's predicament came from its insistence on going back to the gold standard after the war at the highly overvalued pre-war par for the pound, and then insisting on inflating rather than deflating to make its exports competitively priced in the world market. Hence, Britain needed to induce other countries, particularly the U.S., to inflate along with it. The Strong-Norman-Morgan connection did the job, setting the stage for the great financial collapse of 1929–1931.

As World War I drew to a close, influential Britons and Americans decided that intimate post-war collaboration between the two countries required more than just close cooperation between the central banks. Also needed were permanent organizations to promote joint Anglo-American policies to dominate the postwar world.

The Round Table

In England, Cecil Rhodes had launched a secret society in 1891 with the aim of maintaining and expanding the British Empire to re-incorporate the United States. After the turn of the twentieth century, the direction, organization, and expansion of the society fell to Rhodes's friend and executor, Alfred Lord Milner. The Milner Group dominated domestic planning in Britain during World War I, and particularly the planning for post-war foreign and colonial policy. The Milner Group staffed the British delegation of experts to Versailles. To promote the intellectual agitation for such a policy, the Milners had also set up the Round Table Groups in England and abroad in 1910.

The first American to be asked to join the Round Table was George Louis Beer, who came to its attention when his books attacked the American Revolution and praised the British Empire of the eighteenth century. Such loyalty could not go unrewarded, and so Beer became a member of the Group in about 1912 and became the American correspondent of *Round Table* magazine. We have seen Beer's pro-British role as colonial expert for The Inquiry. He was also the chief U.S. expert on colonial affairs at Versailles, and afterward the Milner Group made Beer head of the Mandate Department of the League of Nations.

During the war, Beer, Anglophile Yale historian George Burton Adams, and powerful Columbia University historian James T. Shotwell, an important leader of The Inquiry and head of the

National Board for Historical Services, which emitted deceptive propaganda for the war effort, formed a secret society to promote Anglo-American collaboration. Finally, led by Beer for the United States and the head of the Round Table group in England, Lionel Curtis, the British and U.S. historical staffs at Versailles took the occasion to found a permanent organization to agitate for an informally, if not formally, reconstituted Anglo-American Empire.

The new group, the Institute of International Affairs, was formed at a meeting at the Majestic Hotel in Paris on May 30, 1919. A six-man organizing committee was formed, three Milnerites from Britain, and three Americans: Shotwell; Harvard historian Archibald C. Coolidge, head of the Eastern European desk of the Inquiry, and member of the Morgan-oriented Boston financial family; and James Brown Scott, Morgan lawyer who was to write a biography of Robert Bacon. The British branch, the Royal Institute of International Affairs, set up a committee to supervise writing a multi-volume history of the Versailles Peace Conference; the committee was financed by a gift from Thomas W. Lamont, Morgan partner.

The CFR

The American branch of the new group took a while to get going. Finally, the still inactive American Institute of International Affairs merged with a defunct outfit, begun in 1918, of New York businessmen concerned with the postwar world, and organized as a dinner club to listen to foreign visitors. This organization, the Council on Foreign Relations, had as its honorary chairman Morgan lawyer Elihu Root, while Alexander Hemphill, chairman of Morgan's Guaranty Trust Company, was chairman of its finance committee. In August 1921, the two organizations merged into the new Council on Foreign Relations, Inc., a high-powered organization embracing bankers, lawyers, and intellectuals.

While varied financial interests were represented in the new organization, the CFR was Morgan-dominated, from top to bottom. Honorary president was Elihu Root. President was John W. Davis, Wilson's Solicitor-General, and now chief counsel for J. P. Morgan & Co. Davis was to become Democratic Presidential candidate in 1924. Secretary-Treasurer of the new CFR was Harvard economic historian Edwin F. Gay, director of planning and statistics for the Shipping Board during the war, and now editor of the New York *Evening Post*, owned by his mentor, Morgan partner Thomas W. Lamont.

It was Gay who had the idea of founding *Foreign Affairs*, the CFR's quarterly journal, and who suggested both his Harvard colleague Archibald Coolidge as the first editor, and the

New York Post reporter Hamilton Fish Armstrong as assistant editor and executive director of the CFR. Other prominent officials in the new CFR were: Frank L. Polk, former Under-Secretary of State and now lawyer for J. P. Morgan & Co; Paul M. Warburg of Kuhn, Loeb; Otto H. Kahn of Kuhn, Loeb; former Under-Secretary of State under Wilson, Norman H. Davis, a banking associate of the Morgans; and as vice-president, Paul D. Cravath, senior partner of the Rockefeller-oriented Wall Street law firm of Cravath, Swaine, and Moore.

After World War II, the Council on Foreign Relations became dominated by the Rockefeller rather than by the Morgan interests, a shift of power reflecting a general alteration in financial power in the world at large. After World War II, the rise of oil to prominence brought the Morgans and Rockefellers — once intense rivals — into an Eastern Establishment of which the Rockefellers were the senior, and the Morgans the junior partners.

Rockefeller, Morgan, and War

During the 1930s, the Rockefellers pushed hard for war against Japan, which they saw as competing with them vigorously for oil and rubber resources in Southeast Asia and as endangering the Rockefellers' cherished dreams of a mass "China market" for petroleum products. On the other hand, the Rockefellers took a non-interventionist position in Europe, where they had close financial ties with German firms such as I. G. Farben and Co., and very few close relations with Britain and France. The Morgans, in contrast, as usual deeply committed to their financial ties with Britain and France, once again plumped early for war with Germany, while their interest in the Far East had become minimal. Indeed, U.S. Ambassador to Japan, Joseph C. Grew, former Morgan partner, was one of the few officials in the Roosevelt administration genuinely interested in peace with Japan.

World War II might therefore be considered, from one point of view, as a coalition war: the Morgans got *their* war in Europe, the Rockefellers *theirs* in Asia. Such disgruntled Morgan men as Lewis W. Douglas and Dean G. Acheson (a protégé of Henry Stimson), who had left the early Roosevelt administration in disgust at its soft money policies and economic nationalism, came happily roaring back into government service with the advent of World War II. Nelson A. Rockefeller, for his part, became head of Latin American activities during World War II, and thereby acquired his taste for government service.

After World War II, the united Rockefeller-Morgan-Kuhn, Loeb Eastern Establishment was not allowed to enjoy its financial and political supremacy unchallenged for long. "Cowboy" Sun Belt firms, maverick oil men and construction men from Texas, Florida, and southern California, began to challenge the Eastern Establishment "Yankees" for political power. While both groups favor the Cold War, the Cowboys are more nationalistic, more hawkish, and less inclined to worry about what our European allies are thinking. They are also much less inclined to bail out the now Rockefeller-controlled Chase Manhattan Bank and other Wall Street banks that loaned recklessly to Third World and Communist countries and expect the U.S. taxpayer—through outright taxes or the printing of U.S. dollars—to pick up the tab.

It should be clear that the name of the political party in power is far less important than the particular regime's financial and banking connections. The foreign policy power for so long of Nelson Rockefeller's personal foreign affairs adviser, Henry A. Kissinger, a discovery of the extraordinarily powerful Rocke-feller–Chase Manhattan Bank elder statesman John J. McCloy, is testimony to the importance of financial power. As is the successful lobbying by Kissinger and Chase Manhattan's head, David Rockefeller, to induce Jimmy Carter to allow the ailing Shah of Iran into the U.S.—thus precipitating the humiliating hostage crisis.

Despite differences in nuance, it is clear that Ronald Reagan's originally proclaimed challenge to Rockefeller-Morgan power in the Council of Foreign Relations and to the Rockefeller-created Trilateral Commission has fizzled, and that the "permanent government" continues to rule regardless of the party nominally in power. As a result, the much-heralded "bipartisan foreign policy" consensus imposed by the Establishment since World War II seems to remain safely in place.

David Rockefeller, chairman of the board of his family's Chase Manhattan Bank from 1970 until recently, established the Trilat-eral Commission in 1973, with the financial backing of the CFR and the Rockefeller Foundation. Joseph Kraft, syndicated Washington columnist who himself has the distinction of being both a CFR member and a Trilateralist, has accurately described the CFR as a "school for statesmen," which "comes close to being an organ of what C. Wright Mills has called the Power Elite—a group of men, similar in interest and outlook, shaping events from invulnerable positions behind the scenes." The idea of the Trilateral Commission was to internationalize policy formation, the commission consisting of a small group of multinational corporate leaders, politicians, and foreign policy experts from the U.S., Western Europe, and Japan, who meet to coordinate economic and foreign policy among their respective nations.

Perhaps the most powerful single figure in foreign policy since World War II, a beloved adviser to all Presidents, is the octogenarian John J. McCloy. During World War II, McCloy virtually ran the War Department as Assistant to aging Secretary Stimson; it was McCloy who presided over the decision to round up all Japanese-Americans and place them in concentration camps in World War II, and he is virtually the only American left who still justifies that action.

Before and during the war, McCloy, a disciple of Morgan lawyer Stimson, moved in the Morgan orbit; his brother-in-law, John S. Zinsser, was on the board of directors of J. P. Morgan & Co. during the 1940s. But, reflecting the postwar power shift from Morgan to Rockefeller, McCloy moved quickly into the Rockefeller ambit. He became a partner of the Wall Street corporate law firm of Milbank, Tweed, Hope, Hadley & McCloy, which had long served the Rockefeller family and the Chase Bank as legal counsel.

From there he moved to become Chairman of the Board of the Chase Manhattan Bank, a director of the Rockefeller Foundation, and of Rockefeller Center, Inc., and finally, from 1953 until 1970, chairman of the board of the Council on Foreign Relations. During the Truman administration, McCloy served as President of the World Bank and then U.S. High Commissioner for Germany.

He was also a special adviser to President John F. Kennedy on Disarmament, and chairman of Kennedy's Coordinating Committee on the Cuban Crisis. It was McCloy who "discovered" Professor Henry A. Kissinger for the Rockefeller forces. It is no wonder that John K. Galbraith and Richard Rovere have dubbed McCloy "Mr. Establishment."

A glance at foreign policy leaders since World War II will reveal the domination of the banker elite. Truman's first Secretary of Defense was James V. Forrestal, former president of the investment banking firm of Dillon, Read & Co., closely allied to the Rockefeller financial group. Forrestal had also been a board member of the Chase Securities Corporation, an affiliate of the Chase National Bank.

Another Truman Defense Secretary was Robert A. Lovett, a partner of the powerful New York investment banking house of Brown Brothers Harriman. At the same time that he was Secretary of Defense, Lovett continued to be a trustee of the Rockefeller Foundation. Secretary of the Air Force Thomas K. Finletter was a top Wall Street corporate lawyer and member of the board of the CFR while serving in the cabinet. Ambassador to Soviet Russia, Ambassador to Great Britain, and Secretary of Commerce in the Truman administration was the powerful multi-millionaire W. Averell Harriman, an often underrated but dominant force with the Democratic Party since the days of FDR. Harriman was a partner of Brown Brothers Harriman.

Also Ambassador to Great Britain under Truman was Lewis W. Douglas, brother-in-law of John J. McCloy, a trustee of the Rockefeller Foundation, and a board member of the Council on Foreign Relations. Following Douglas as Ambassador to the Court of St. James was Walter S. Gifford, chairman of the board of AT&T, and member of the board of trustees of the Rockefeller Foundation for almost two decades. Ambassador to NATO under Truman was William H. Draper, Jr., vice-president of Dillon, Read & Co.

Also influential in helping the Truman administration organize the Cold War was director of the policy planning staff of the State Department, Paul H. Nitze. Nitze, whose wife was a member of the Pratt family, associated with the Rockefeller family since the origins of Standard Oil, had been vice-president of Dillon, Read & Co.

When Truman entered the Korean War, he created an Office of Defense Mobilization to run the domestic economy during the war. The first director was Charles E. ("Electric Charlie") Wilson, president of the Morgan-controlled General Electric Company, who also served as board member of the Morgans' Guaranty Trust Company. His two most influential assistants were Sidney J. Weinberg, ubiquitous senior partner in the Wall Street investment banking firm of Goldman Sachs & Co., and former General Lucius D. Clay, chairman of the board of Continental Can Co., and a director of the Lehman Corporation.

Succeeding McCloy as President of the World Bank, and continuing in that post throughout the two terms of Dwight Eisenhower, was Eugene Black. Black had served for fourteen years as vice-president of the Chase National Bank, and was persuaded to take the World Bank post by the bank's chairman of the board, Winthrop W. Aldrich, brother-in-law of John D. Rockefeller, Jr. The Eisenhower administration proved to be a field day for the Rockefeller interests. While president of Columbia University, Eisenhower was invited to high-level dinners where he met and was groomed for President by top leaders from the Rockefeller and Morgan ambits, including the chairman of the board of Rockefeller's Standard Oil of New Jersey, the presidents of six other big oil companies, including Standard of California and Socony-Vacuum, and the executive vice-president of J. P. Morgan & Co.

One dinner was hosted by Clarence Dillon, the multi-millionaire retired founder of Dillon, Read & Co., where the guests included Russell B. Leffingwell, chairman of the board of both J. P. Morgan & Co. and the CFR (before McCloy); John M. Schiff, a senior partner of the investment banking house of Kuhn, Loeb & Co.; the financier Jeremiah Milbank, a director of the Chase Manhattan Bank; and John D. Rockefeller, Jr. Even earlier, during 1949,

Eisenhower had been introduced through a special study group to key figures in the CFR. The study group devised a plan to create a new organization called the American Assembly—in essence an expanded CFR study group—whose main function was reputedly to build up Eisenhower's prospects for the Presidency. A leader of the "Citizens for Eisenhower" committee, who later became Ike's Ambassador to Great Britain, was the multi-millionaire John Hay Whitney, scion of several wealthy families, whose granduncle, Oliver H. Payne, had been one of the associates of John D. Rockefeller, Sr. in founding the Standard Oil Company. Whitney was head of his own investment concern, J. H. Whitney & Co., and later became publisher of the *New York Herald Tribune.*

Running foreign policy during the Eisenhower administration was the Dulles family, led by Secretary of State John Foster Dulles, who had also concluded the U.S. peace treaty with Japan under Harry Truman. Dulles had for three decades been a senior partner of the top Wall Street corporate law firm of Sullivan & Cromwell, whose most important client was Rockefeller's Standard Oil Company of New Jersey. Dulles had been for fifteen years a member of the board of the Rockefeller Foundation, and before assuming the post of Secretary of State was chairman of the board of that institution. Most important is the little-known fact that Dulles's wife was Janet Pomeroy Avery, a first cousin of John D. Rockefeller, Jr. Heading the super-secret Central Intelligence Agency during the Eisenhower years was Dulles's brother, Allen Welsh Dulles, also a partner in Sullivan & Cromwell. Allen Dulles had long been a trustee of the CFR and had served as its president from 1947 to 1951. Their sister, Eleanor Lansing Dulles, was head of the Berlin desk of the State Department during that decade.

Under-Secretary of State, and the man who succeeded John Foster Dulles in the spring 1959, was former Massachusetts Governor Christian A. Herter. Herter's wife, like Nitze's, was a member of the Pratt family. Indeed, his wife's uncle, Herbert L. Pratt, had been for many years president or chairman of the board of Standard Oil Company of New York. One of Mrs. Herter's cousins, Richardson Pratt, had served as assistant treasurer of Standard Oil of New Jersey up to 1945. Furthermore, one of Herter's own uncles, a physician, had been for many years treasurer of the Rockefeller Institute for Medical Research.

Herter was succeeded as Under-Secretary of State by Eisenhower's Ambassador to France, C. Douglas Dillon, son of Clarence, and himself Chairman of the Board of Dillon, Read & Co. Dillon was soon to become a trustee of the Rockefeller Foundation.

Perhaps to provide some balance for his banker-business coalition, Eisenhower appointed as Secretary of Defense three men in the Morgan rather than the Rockefeller ambit. Charles B. ("Engine Charlie") Wilson was president of General Motors, member of the board of J. P. Morgan & Co. Wilson's successor, Neil H. McElroy, was president of Proctor & Gamble Co. His board chairman, R. R. Deupree, was also a director of J. P. Morgan & Co. The third Secretary of Defense who had been Under-Secretary and Secretary of the Navy under Eisenhower, was Thomas S. Gates, Jr., who had been a partner of the Morgan-connected Philadelphia investment banking firm of Drexel & Co. When Gates stepped down as Defense Secretary, he became president of the newly formed flagship commercial bank for the Morgan interests, the Morgan Guaranty Trust Co.

Serving as Secretary of the Navy and then Deputy Secretary of Defense (and later Secretary of the Treasury) under Eisenhower was Texas businessman Robert B. Anderson. After leaving the Defense Department, Anderson became a board member of the Rockefeller-controlled American Overseas Investing Co., and, before becoming Secretary of the Treasury, he borrowed $84,000 from Nelson A. Rockefeller to buy stock in Nelson's International Basic Economy Corporation.

Head of the important Atomic Energy Commission during the Eisenhower years was Lewis L. Strauss. For two decades, Strauss had been a partner in the investment banking firm of Kuhn, Loeb & Co. In 1950, Strauss had become financial adviser to the Rockefeller family, soon also becoming a board member of Rockefeller Center, Inc.

A powerful force in deciding foreign policy was the National Security Council, which included on it the Dulles brothers, Strauss, and Wilson. Particularly important is the post of national security adviser to the President. Eisenhower's first national security adviser was Robert Cutler, president of the Old Colony Trust Co., the largest trust operation outside New York City. The Old Colony was a trust affiliate of the First National Bank of Boston.

After two years in the top national security post, Cutler returned to Boston to become chairman of the board of Old Colony Trust, returning after a while to the national security slot for two more years. In between, Eisenhower had two successive national security advisers. The first was Dillon Anderson, a Houston corporate attorney, who did work for several oil companies. Particularly significant was Anderson's position as chairman of the board of a small but fascinating Connecticut firm called Electro-Mechanical Research, Inc. Electro-Mechanical was closely associated with certain Rockefeller financiers; thus, one of its directors was Godfrey Rockefeller, a limited partner in the investment banking firm of Clark, Dodge & Co.

After more than a year, Anderson resigned from his national security post and was replaced by William H. Jackson, a partner of the investment firm of J. H. Whitney & Co. Before assuming his powerful position, Dillon Anderson had been one of several men serving as special hush-hush consultants to the National Security Council. Another special adviser was Eugene Holman, president of Rockefeller's Standard Oil Company of New Jersey.

We may mention two important foreign policy actions of the Eisenhower administration which seem to reflect the striking influence of personnel directly tied to bankers and financial interests. In 1951, the regime of Mohammed Mossadegh in Iran decided to nationalize the British-owned oil holdings of the Anglo-Iranian Oil company. It took no time for the newly established Eisenhower administration to intervene heavily in this situation.

CIA director and former Standard Oil lawyer Allen W. Dulles flew to Switzerland to organize the covert overthrow of the Mossadegh regime, the throwing of Mossadegh into prison, and the restoration of the Shah to the throne of Iran.

After lengthy behind-the-scenes negotiations, the oil industry was put back into action as purchasers and refiners of Iranian oil. But this time the picture was significantly different. Instead of the British getting all of the oil pie, their share was reduced to 40 percent of the new oil consortium, with five top U.S. oil companies (Standard Oil of New Jersey, Socony-Vacuum—formerly Standard Oil of N.Y., and now Mobil—Standard Oil of California, Gulf, and Texaco) getting another 40 percent.

It was later disclosed that Secretary of State Dulles placed a sharp upper limit on any participation in the consortium by smaller independent oil companies in the United States. In addition to the rewards to the Rockefeller interests, the CIA's man-on-the-spot directing the operation, Kermit Roosevelt, received his due by quickly becoming a vice-president of Mellon's Gulf Oil Corp.

The Guatemalan Coup

Fresh from its CIA triumph in Iran, the Eisenhower administration next turned its attention to Guatemala, where the left-liberal regime of Jacob Arbenz Guzman had nationalized 234,000 acres of uncultivated land owned by the nation's largest landholder, the American-owned United Fruit Company, which imported about 60 percent of all bananas coming into the United States.

Arbenz also announced his intention of seizing another 173,000 acres of idle United Fruit land along the Caribbean coast. In late 1953, Eisenhower gave the CIA the assignment of organizing a counter-revolution in Guatemala. With the actual operation directed by former Wall Street corporate lawyer Frank Wisner of the CIA, the agency launched a successful invasion of Guatemala, led by exiled Army Colonel Castilo Armas, which soon overthrew the Arbenz regime and replaced it with a military junta. The Arbenz land program was abolished, and most of its expropriated property was returned to the United Fruit Company.

Allen W. Dulles had financial connections with United Fruit and with various sugar companies which had also suffered land expropriation from the Arbenz regime. For several years, while a partner at Sullivan & Cromwell, he had been a board member of the Rockefeller-controlled J. Henry Schroder Banking Corporation. Members of the board of Schroder during 1953 included Delano Andrews, Sullivan & Cromwell partner who had taken Dulles's seat on the board; George A. Braga, president of the

Manati Sugar Company; Charles W. Gibson, vice-president of the Rockefeller-affiliated Air Reduction Company; and Avery Rockefeller, president of the closely linked banking house of Schroder, Rockefeller, & Co. Members of the board of Manati Sugar, in the meanwhile, included Alfred Jaretski, Jr., another Sullivan & Cromwell partner; Gerald F. Beal, president of J. Henry Schroder and chairman of the board of the International Railways of Central America; and Henry E. Worcester, a recently retired of executive of United Fruit.

United Fruit, furthermore, was a controlling shareholder in International Railways, while, as in the case of Beal, the board chairmanship of the railway had long been held by a high official of Schroder. The close ties between United Fruit, Schroder, and International Railways may also be seen by the fact that, in 1959, the board chairman of the railway became James McGovern, general counsel for United Fruit. International Railway, in fact, carried most of United Fruit's produce from the interior to the port in Guatemala. In addition, Dulles's close associate and fellow trustee of the Council of Foreign Relations in this period, and former treasurer of the CFR, was Whitney H. Shepardson, formerly vice-president of International Railways.

Not only that: Robert Cutler, national security adviser to the President at the time of the coup against Arbenz, had himself very close ties to United Fruit. Cutler's boss at Old Colony Trust, chairman of the board T. Jefferson Coolidge, was also, and more importantly, board chairman at United Fruit. Indeed, many members of the board of United Fruit, a Boston-based company, were also on the board of Old Colony or its mother company, the First National Bank of Boston.

Furthermore, during the period of planning the Guatemalan coup, and up till a few months before its success in 1954, the Assistant Secretary of State for Inter-American Affairs was John Moors Cabot, a well-known anti-Arbenz hawk. Cabot's brother Thomas D., was an executive of United Fruit and a member of the board of the First National Bank of Boston.

The Council on Foreign Relations played an important role in the Guatemalan invasion. It began in the fall of 1952, when Spruille Braden, a former Assistant Secretary of State for Inter-American Affairs and then consultant for United Fruit, led a CFR study group on Political Unrest in Latin America. Discussion leader at the first meeting of the CFR-Braden group was John McClintock, an executive of United Fruit. Former leading New Dealer and Assistant Secretary of State Adolf A. Berle, Jr., a participant in the study group, recorded in his diary that the U.S. should welcome an overthrow of the Arbenz government, and noted that, "I am arranging to see Nelson Rockefeller (himself Assistant Secretary of State for Inter-American Affairs during World War II) who knows the situation and can work a little with General Eisenhower."

In the actual Guatemalan operation, President Eisenhower himself was a CFR member, as were Allen Dulles, John M. Cabot and Frank Wisner, the man in charge of the coup and the CIA's deputy director for plans. Of the twelve people in the U.S. government identified as being involved at the top level in the Guatemalan affair, eight were CFR members or would be within a few years. These included, in addition to the above, Henry F. Holland, who succeeded Cabot in the assistant secretary of state slot in 1954; Under-Secretary of State Walter Bedell Smith, a former director of the CIA; and Ambassador to the UN Henry Cabot Lodge.

Paving the way for the coup was a public report, issued in December 1953 by the Committee on International Policy of the National Planning Association on the Guatemalan situation. Head of the Committee was Frank Altschul, secretary and vice-president of the CFR and a partner of the international banking house of Lazard Frères, as well as a director of the Chase National Bank and president of the General American Investor Corp., a firm largely controlled by Lehman Brothers. The Altschul report, signed by twenty-two committee members of whom fifteen were CFR members, warned that "Communist infiltration in Guatemala" was a threat to the security of the Western Hemisphere and hinted that drastic action would probably be necessary to deal with this menace.

Of those involved in the drastic action, Secretary of State John Foster Dulles, while at Sullivan & Cromwell, had once represented United Fruit in negotiating a contract with Guatemala. Under-Secretary of State Walter Bedell Smith, after leaving the government, became director of United Fruit, as did Robert D. Hill, who participated in the Guatemala operation as Ambassador to Costa Rica. Furthermore, future president of Guatemala Miguel Ydigoras Fuentes noted that his own cooperation in the coup against Arbenz was obtained by Walter Turnbull, a former executive at United Fruit, who came to him along with two CIA agents.

JFK and the Establishment

When John F. Kennedy assumed the office of President, the first person he turned to for foreign policy advice was Robert A. Lovett, partner of Brown Brothers, Harriman, even though Lovett had backed Richard Nixon. Kennedy asked Lovett to take his pick of any of three top jobs in the Cabinet—State, Defense, and Treasury—but the ill and aging Lovett demurred. It was at Lovett's urging, however, that Kennedy chose as Secretary of State Dean Rusk, president of the Rockefeller Foundation, a post he had acquired because of the strong backing of John Foster Dulles. Under-Secretary of State was Chester Bowles, a trustee of the Rockefeller Foundation; Bowles was soon replaced by corporate lawyer George Bail, who was later to become a senior managing partner at Lehman Brothers.

For Secretary of Defense Kennedy chose Robert S. McNamara, President of Ford Motor Company. One influential force in the McNamara appointment was the backing of Sidney J. Weinberg, partner of the investment banking firm of Goldman, Sachs, & Co. and powerful fund-raiser for the Democratic Party. Weinberg was a member of the board of Ford Motor Company. Perhaps even more important was the intimate Ford connection with the investment banking house of Lehman Brothers, which had long carried great weight in the party; at that time, five high-ranking Ford executives sat on the board of the One William Street Fund, a mutual fund recently established by Lehman Brothers.

Secretary of the Air Force was Eugene Zuckert, chairman of the board of the small Pittsburgh firm, the Nuclear Science and Engineering Corp., controlled by the powerful Lehman Brothers. Before going to this firm, Zuckert had been a member of the Atomic Energy Commission; former ABC Commissioner Gordon Dean, who had preceded Zuckert as chairman of the board of Nuclear Science and Engineering, was also a partner of Lehman Brothers.

General counsel of the Defense Department, and soon to become Secretary of the Army, was Wall Street corporate lawyer Cyrus Vance, later to become Secretary of State under Carter. Vance's law firm—Simpson, Thacher & Bartlett—represented Lehman Brothers and Manufacturers Hanover Trust Co. Moreover, Vance had married into New York's wealthy W. & J. Sloane family; his father-in-law, John Sloane, had served as a director of the United States Trust Co.

Secretary of the Treasury in the Kennedy Cabinet was C. Douglas Dillon, of Dillon, Read and the Rockefeller Foundation. Dillon saw no problem in serving for eight years as Ambassador to France and as a State Department official during the Eisenhower Era, and then segueing to the Democratic Kennedy Cabinet. Like Lovett, he too was chosen even though he had been a big contributor to the Nixon effort of 1960.

In the powerful post of National Security Adviser, Kennedy selected Harvard Dean McGeorge Bundy, who had been part of a high-powered foreign policy team advising Thomas B. Dewey in the 1948 campaign, a virtually all-Rockefeller dominated team headed by John Foster Dulles and including Dulles's brother Allen, C. Douglas Dillon, and Christian Herter. After that, Bundy worked for the Council on Foreign Relations.

Bundy had been born into the wealthy Boston Brahmin Lowell family, his mother having been a Lowell. His father Harvey H. Bundy, was a partner in Boston's top law firm of Choate, Hall & Stewart, a high official of the Foreign Bondholders Protective Council, and a director of the Merchants National Bank of Boston. McGeorge's brother, William, a high CIA official, was married to the daughter of former Secretary of State Dean Acheson, and his sister Katherine married into the socially prominent Auch-inchloss family, the family of Jacqueline Kennedy.

The strong Rockefeller influence on Kennedy foreign policy is best seen in the fact that the new President continued Allen W. Dulles as head of the CIA. It was at the urging of Dulles that Kennedy decided to go ahead with the CIA's previously planned and disastrous Bay of Pigs invasion of Cuba. Fidel Castro's regime had recently nationalized a large number of American-owned sugar companies in Cuba. It might be noted that Dulles's old law firm of Sullivan & Cromwell served as general counsel for two of these large sugar companies, the Francisco Sugar Co. and the Manati Sugar Co., and that one of the board members of these firms was Gerald F. Beal, president of the Rockefeller-oriented J. Henry Schroder Bank, of which Dulles had once been a director.

Not only that. John L. Loeb of the Loeb, Rhoades investment bank, whose wife was a member of the Lehman banking family, owned a large block of stock in the nationalized Compania Azucarera Atlantica del Golfo, a big sugar plantation in Cuba, while one of the directors of the latter company was Harold F. Linder, vice-chairman of the General American Investors Company, dominated by Lehman Brothers and Lazard Frères investment bankers. Linder was appointed head of the Export-Import Bank by President Kennedy.

After the Bay of Pigs fiasco, Dulles was replaced as head of the CIA by West Coast industrialist John A. McCone, who also had the capacity to serve the administrations of either party with equal ease. Under-Secretary of the Air Force under Truman and head of the Atomic Energy Commission under Eisenhower, Mc-Cone was president of the Bechtel-McCone Corporation, and represents the first major incursion of the international Bechtel construction interests into American politics. McCone was also a board member of the California Bank of Los Angeles, and of the Rockefeller-dominated Standard Oil Company of California.

The CIA was also heavily involved about this time in the short-lived Katanga secession movement in the old Belgian Congo. One of the largest of the American companies in Katanga, and a major backer of the secession movement, was the Anglo-American Corporation of South Africa, one of whose partners was mining magnate Charles W. Engelhard. Engelhard's investment banker was Dillon, Read, the family firm of Kennedy's Secretary of the Treasury, C. Douglas Dillon.

We have seen that Mr. Establishment, the Rockefeller-oriented John J. McCloy, served as Kennedy's special adviser on disarmament. When the U.S. Arms Control and Disarmament Agency was created in the fall of 1961, its first head was William C. Foster, former Under-Secretary of State and Defense under Truman. In between, Foster had served as a high official of the Olin Mathieson Chemical Corp., and then board chairman of the Rockefeller-dominated United Nuclear Corp. Foster was also a director of the CFR.

Kennedy continued Rockefeller's Eugene Black as head of the powerful World Bank. When Black reached retirement age in 1962, he was replaced by George D. Woods, chairman of the board of the prominent investment bank, First Boston Corporation. Woods had many connections with the Rockefeller interests, including being a director of the Chase International Investment Corp., of the Rockefeller Foundation, and of other Rockefeller-dominated concerns.

Two important foreign policy actions of the Kennedy administration were the Cuban Missile Crisis and the escalation of the war in Vietnam. Kennedy was advised during the Cuban missile crisis by an *ad hoc* group called the Ex Comm, which included, along with his official major foreign policy advisers, Robert A. Lovett and John J. McCloy. In the Vietnam War, Kennedy brought in as Ambassador to South Vietnam the Boston Brahmin and Morgan-oriented Henry Cabot Lodge, who had been Eisenhower's Ambassador to the United Nations and who had run for Vice-President on the Nixon ticket in 1960. Virtually the last foreign policy act of John F. Kennedy was to give the green light to Lodge and the CIA to oust, and murder, South Vietnamese President Ngô Đình Diệm.

LBJ and the Power Elite

Lyndon Johnson's foreign policy was dominated by his escalation of the Vietnam conflict into a full-scale (if undeclared) war, and of the increasing splits over the war among the financial power elite. Johnson retained the hawkish Rusk, McNamara, McCone, and Lodge in their posts. As newly minted Vietnam doves were ousted from foreign policy positions, they were replaced by hawks. Thus, William Bundy became Assistant Secretary of State for Far Eastern Affairs, at the same time becoming a director of the CFR. On the other hand, the increasingly critical W. Averell Harriman was ousted from his post of Under-Secretary of State.

Cyrus Vance continued as Johnson's Secretary of the Army; when he rose to Deputy Secretary of Defense, he was replaced by Vance's old friend and roommate at Yale, Stanley R. Resor. Resor was a partner in the major Wall Street law firm of Debevoise, Plimpton, Lyons, & Gates, and was the brother-in-law of economist and banker Gabriel Hauge, president of the Manufacturers Hanover Trust, and treasurer of the CFR.

Resor had married into the Pillsbury flour family of Minneapolis, which had long been connected with the holding company, the Northwest Bancorporation. After Vance retired as Deputy Secretary of Defense to return to law practice, he was replaced by Johnson's hard-line Secretary of the Navy Paul Nitze, former partner of Dillon, Read, whose wife was a member of the Rockefeller-connected Pratt family.

One important meeting at which it was decided to escalate the Vietnam War was held in July 1965. The meeting consisted of Johnson, his designated foreign policy and military officials, and three key unofficial advisers: Clark M. Clifford, the chairman of the President's Foreign Intelligence Advisory Board, and an attorney for the du Ponts and the Morgan-dominated General Electric Co.; Arthur H. Dean, a partner in Rockefeller-oriented Sullivan & Cromwell and a director of the CFR; and the ubiquitous John J. McCloy.

Shortly after the meeting, a distinguished national committee of power elite figures was formed to back President Johnson's aggressive policies in Vietnam. Chairman of the committee was Arthur H. Dean; other members were Dean Acheson; Eugene Black, who, after retiring as head of the World Bank, returned to be a director of Chase Manhattan; Gabriel Hauge of Manufacturers' Trust and the CFR; David Rockefeller, president of the Chase Manhattan Bank and a vice-president of the CFR; and two board members of AT&T, William B. Murphy and James R. Killian, Jr. Indeed, of the 46 members of this pro-Vietnam War committee, 19 were prominent businessmen, bankers or corporate lawyers. Later, when Johnson needed to raise taxes to supply more funds for the war effort, he selected thirteen businessmen to head the lobbying effort.

A fascinating aspect of the Johnson administration was the heavy influence of men connected with the powerful Democratic investment banking house of Lehman Brothers. Johnson's first Under-Secretary of State, George Ball, who left because of increasing disillusionment with the Vietnam War, would later become a key partner of Lehman Brothers. Johnson's most influential unofficial adviser was long-time and personal legal and financial adviser Edwin L. Weisl, a New York attorney who was a senior law partner to Cyrus Vance at Simpson, Thacher & Bartlett. Not only was this law firm the general counsel to Lehman Brothers, but Weisl himself was dubbed by *Fortune* magazine as "Lehman's eighteenth partner." Weisl had great influence at Lehman and occasionally sat in on partners' meetings. He was also reputed to be the closest friend of senior partner Robert Lehman, and sat on the board of the Lehman-controlled One William Street Fund.

Another very close and influential Johnson adviser, and a consistent hard-liner on Vietnam, was his old friend Abe Fortas, a Washington lawyer and veteran New Dealer. During the Johnson years, Fortas served as director, vice-president, and general counsel for the Texas-based GreatAmerica Corp., a giant holding company controlling several insurance companies, Braniff Airways, and two banks, including the First Western Bank and Trust Co. of California.

During the same period, Fortas was also a director and vice-president of the large Federated Department Stores. Both Federated and GreatAmerica had close ties with Lehman Brothers. Fred Lazarus, Jr., a top official of Federated, sat on the board of the Lehman-controlled One William Street Fund, along with Edwin Weisl. And the only two non-Texans on the board of GreatAmerica Corp. were William H. Osborn, Jr., of Lehman Brothers, and Gustave L. Levy, a partner in the closely allied Wall Street investment bank of Goldman, Sachs & Co. Goldman, Sachs was the senior banking adviser for the Murchison Texas oil interests, a group with whom Lyndon Johnson was personally allied.

Finally, after Henry Cabot Lodge retired as the hawkish Ambassador to South Vietnam in 1967, he was replaced by Ellsworth Bunker. Bunker, who had been president of the National Sugar Refining Company, served as ambassador to various countries in the Eisenhower administration, and then Ambassador to the Organization of American States under Johnson. Bunker was connected to John L. Loeb, the Lehman kinsman who headed the investment banking firm of Carl M. Loeb, Rhoades & Co. Loeb placed Bunker on the board of Curtis Publishing Co. after he obtained control of that firm for Loeb, Rhoades. Loeb also installed Bunker's son, John, as president of Curtis. Furthermore, Ellsworth Bunker's younger brother, Arthur, had served as director of the Lehman Corporation, and of Lehman's One William Street Fund until his death in 1964.

While Bunker had served Johnson as Ambassador to the OAS, he continued to sit on the board of the National Sugar Refining Company. In late 1965, Bunker played a crucial role in Johnson's massive U.S. invasion of the Dominican Republic, an intervention into a Dominican civil war to prevent a victory by left-wing forces who would presumably pose a dire threat to American sugar companies in the republic. As President Johnson's emissary to the Dominican Republic just after the invasion, Bunker played a decisive role in installing the conservative Hector Garcia-Godoy as president.

Increasingly, however, the power elite became divided over the morass of the Vietnam War. Under the blows of the Tet offensive in January 1968, Robert McNamara had become increasingly dovish and was replaced as Secretary of Defense by hard-liner Clark Clifford, with McNamara moving gracefully to take charge of the World Bank. But, on investigating the situation, Clifford, too, became critical of the war, and Johnson called a crucial two-day meeting on March 22, 1968, of his highly influential Senior Informal Advisory Group on Vietnam, known as the "Wise Men," made up of all his key advisors on foreign affairs.

Johnson was stunned to find that only Abe Fortas and General Maxwell Taylor continued in the hard-line position. Arthur Dean, Cabot Lodge, John J. McCloy, and former General Omar Bradley took a confused middle-of-the-road position, while all the other elite figures such as Dean Acheson, George Ball, McGeorge Bundy, C. Douglas Dillon, and Cyrus Vance had swung around to a firm opposition to the war.

As David Halberstam put it in his *The Best and the Brightest*, these power elite leaders "let him (Johnson) know that the Establishment—yes, Wall Street—had turned on the war.... It was hurting the economy, dividing the country, turning the youth against the country's best traditions." LBJ knew when he was licked. Only a few days afterward, Johnson announced that he was not going to run for re-election and he ordered what would be the beginnings of U.S. disengagement from Vietnam.

The foreign-policy aims of the Nixon administration had a decided Rockefeller stamp. Secretary of State William P. Rogers was a Wall Street lawyer who had long been active in the liberal Dewey-Rockefeller wing of the New York Republican Party. Indeed, Thomas E. Dewey was the main backer of Rogers for the State Department post.

Dewey's entire political career was beholden to the Rockefeller interests, as was dramatically shown one election year when, in an incident that received unaccustomed publicity, Winthrop W. Aldrich, Rockefeller kinsman who was president of the Chase National Bank, literally ordered Governor Dewey into his Wall Street offices and commanded him to run for re-election. The governor, who had previously announced his retirement into private practice, meekly obeyed. Furthermore, Roger's law partner, John A. Wells, had long been one of Nelson Rockefeller's top political aides and had served as Nelson's campaign manager for President in 1964.

Second-tier posts in the Nixon State Department went to financial elite figures. Thus, the following men were successively Under Secretaries of State (after 1972, Deputy Secretaries) in the Nixon White House:

• Elliot L. Richardson, partner of a Boston Brahmin corporate law firm and a director of the New England Trust Co., and a man whose uncle, Henry L. Shattuck, had long been a director of the New England Merchants National Bank and of the Mutual Life Insurance Co. of New York.

• John N. Irwin II, partner of a Wall St. law firm (Patterson, Belknap & Webb) long associated with the Rockefeller interests, and whose wife was a sister of the Watson brothers family of IBM.

• Kenneth Rush, president of Union Carbide Corp., and a director of the Bankers Trust Co. of New York.

• Robert S. Ingersoll, chairman of the board of Borg-Warner Corp. and a director of the First National Bank of Chicago.

Also, the Deputy Under-Secretary of State for Economic Affairs under Nixon was Nathaniel Samuels, a partner in the investment banking house of Kuhn, Loeb & Co., and a director of the Rockefeller-controlled International Basic Economy Corp.

Henry A. Kissinger

But of course the dominant foreign policy figure in both the Nixon and Ford administrations was not William Rogers but Henry A. Kissinger, who was named national security adviser and soon became virtually the sole force in foreign policy, officially replacing Rogers as Secretary of State in 1973.

Kissinger was virtually "Mr. Rockefeller." As a Harvard political scientist, Kissinger had been discovered by John J. McCloy, and made director of a CFR group to study the Soviet threat in the nuclear age. He was soon made director of a special foreign policy studies project of the Rockefeller Brothers Fund, and from there became for more than a decade Nelson Rockefeller's chief personal foreign policy adviser.

Only three days before accepting the Nixon administration post, Rockefeller gave Kissinger $50,000 to ease the fiscal burdens of his official post. Nixon and Kissinger re-escalated the Vietnam War by secretly bombing and then invading Cambodia in 1969 and 1970; they could be sure of compliance from Ellsworth Bunker, whom Nixon retained as Ambassador to South Vietnam until the end of the war.

Apart from the Vietnam War, the Nixon administration's major foreign policy venture was the CIA-led overthrow of the Marxist Allende regime in Chile. U.S. firms controlled about 80 percent of Chile's copper production, and copper was by far Chile's major export. In the 1970 election, the CIA funneled $1 million into Chile in an unsuccessful attempt to defeat Allende. The new Allende regime then proceeded to nationalize large U.S.-owned firms, including Anaconda and Kennecott Copper and the Chile Telephone Co., a large utility which was a subsidiary of ITT (International Telephone and Telegraph Co.).

Under the advice of Henry Kissinger and of ITT, the CIA funneled $8 million into Chile over the next three years, in an ultimately successful effort to overthrow the Allende regime. Particularly helpful in this effort was John A. McCone, the West Coast industrialist whom Johnson had continued in charge of the CIA. Now a board member of ITT, McCone continued in constant contact by being named a consultant to the CIA on the Chilean question. President Nixon continued Johnson holdover Richard Helms as head of the CIA, and Helm's outlook may have been influenced by the fact that his grandfather, Gates W. McGarrah, had been the head of the Mechanics and Metals National Bank of New York, director of Bankers Trust, and chairman of the board of the powerful Federal Reserve Bank of New York.

Of the $8 million poured into Chile by the CIA, over $1.5 million was allocated to Chile's largest opposition newspaper, *El Mercurio*, published by wealthy businessman Augustin Edwards. Edwards was also, not coincidentally, vice president of Pepsico, a company headed by President Nixon's close friend Donald M. Kendall. The transaction was arranged at a quiet breakfast meeting in Washington, set up by Kendall, and including Edwards and Henry Kissinger. After the successful overthrow of Allende by a military junta in September 1973, the man who became the first Minister of Economy, Development, and Reconstruction was Fernando Leniz, a high official of *El Mercurio* who also served on the board of the Chilean subsidiary of the Rockefeller-controlled International Basic Economy Corporation.

Richard Nixon also established, for the first time, diplomatic relations with Communist China. Nixon was urged to take this step by a committee of prominent businessmen and financiers interested in promoting trade with and investments in China. The group included Kendall; Gabriel Hauge, chairman of Manufacturers Hanover Trust Co.; Donald Burnham, head of Westinghouse; and David Rockefeller, chairman of the Chase Manhattan Bank.

The first envoy to China was the veteran elite figure and diplomat, David K. E. Bruce, who had married a Mellon, and who had served in high diplomatic posts in every administration since that of Harry Truman. After Bruce became Ambassador to NATO, he was replaced by George H. W. Bush, a Texas oil man who had served briefly as Ambassador to the United Nations. More important than Bush's Texas oil connections was the fact that his father, Connecticut Senator Prescott Bush, was a partner at Brown Brothers, Harriman.

The Trilateral Commission

In July 1973 a development occurred which was to have a critical impact on U.S. foreign—and domestic—policy. David Rockefeller formed the Trilateral Commission, as a more elite and exclusive organization than the CFR, and containing statesmen, businessmen, and intellectuals from Western Europe and Japan.

The Trilateral Commission not only studied and formulated policy, but began to place its people in top governmental posts. North American secretary and coordinator for the Trilaterals was George S. Franklin, Jr., who had been for many years executive director of the CFR. Franklin had been David Rockefeller's roommate in college and had married Helena Edgell, a cousin of Rockefeller. Henry Kissinger was of course a key member of the Trilaterals, and its staff director was Columbia University political scientist Zbigniew Brzezinski, who was also a recently selected director of the CFR.

President Ford continued Kissinger as his Secretary of State and top foreign policy director. Kissinger's leading aide during the Ford years was Robert S. Ingersoll, Trilateralist from Borg-Warner Corp. and the First National Bank of Chicago. In 1974, Ingersoll was replaced as Deputy Secretary of State by Charles W. Robinson, a businessman and Trilateralist.

Ambassador to Great Britain—and then moved to several other posts—was Elliot Richardson, now a Trilateralist and a director of the CFR. George Bush, Trilateralist, was retained as

Ambassador to China, and then became director of the CIA. He was replaced as Ambassador by Thomas S. Gates, Jr., head of the Morgans' flagship bank, Morgan Guaranty Trust Co. Meanwhile, Robert McNamara continued to head the World Bank. Becoming head of the Export-Import Bank in 1975 was Stephen M. DuBrul, Jr., who had had the distinction of being a partner of both Lehman Brothers and Lazard Frères.

James Earl Carter and his administration were virtually complete creatures of the Trilateral Commission. In the early 1970s, the financial elite was looking for a likely liberal Southern governor who might be installed in the White House. They were considering Reubin Askew and Terry Sanford, but they settled on the obscure Georgia governor, Jimmy Carter. They were aided in their decision by the fact that Jimmy came highly recommended.

In the first place, it must be realized that "Atlanta" has for decades meant Coca-Cola, the great multi-billion dollar corporation which has long stood at the center of Atlanta's politico-economic power elite. Jimmy Carter's long-time attorney, close personal friend, and political mentor was Charles Kirbo, senior partner at Atlanta's top corporate law firm of King & Spalding.

King & Spalding had long been the general counsel to Coca-Cola, and also to the mighty financial firm The Trust Co. of Georgia, long known in Atlanta as "the Coca-Cola bank." The long-time head and major owner of Coca-Cola was the octogenerian Robert W. Woodruff, who had long been highly influential in Georgia politics. With Kirbo at his elbow, Jimmy Carter soon gained the whole-hearted political backing of the Coca-Cola interests.

Financial contributors to Carter's race in the 1971 Democratic primary for governor were: John Paul Austin, powerful chairman of the board of Coca-Cola; and three vice-presidents of Coke, including Joseph W. Jones, the personal assistant to Robert Woodruff. If Pepsi was a Republican firm, Coke had long been prominent in the Democratic Party; thus, James A. Farley, long-time head of the Democratic National Committee, was for thirty-five years head of the Coca-Cola Export Company.

In 1971, Carter was introduced to David Rockefeller by the latter's friend J. Paul Austin, who was to become a founding member of the Trilateral Commission. Austin was long connected with the Morgan interests, and served as a director of the Morgan Guaranty Trust Co., and of Morgan's General Electric Co. Other early political backers of Jimmy Carter were the Gambrell brothers, David and E. Smyth, of a family which was a major stockholder in Rockefeller-controlled Eastern Air Lines. The Gambrell law firm, indeed, served as the general counsel for Eastern. They, too, aided in forming the Carter-Rockefeller connection.

During the same period, Carter was also introduced to the powerful Hedley Donovan, editor-in-chief of *Time* magazine, who was also to be a founding Trilateralist. Rockefeller and Donovan liked what they saw, and Carter was also recommended to the Trilaterals by the Atlanta Committee of the Council on Foreign Relations.

Jimmy Carter was invited to become a member of the Trilateral Commission shortly after it was formed, and he agreed enthusiastically. Why did the Trilaterals appoint an obscure Georgia governor with admittedly no knowledge of foreign affairs? Ostensibly because they wanted to hear the views of a Southern governor. Far more likely, they were grooming him for the Presidency and wanted to instruct him in trilateralism. Carter took instruction well, and he wrote later of the many happy hours he spent sitting at the feet of Trilateral executive director and international relations expert Zbigniew Brzezinski.

What the unknown Carter needed more than even money for his 1975–1976 campaign for President was extensive and favorable media exposure. He received it from the Trilateral-influenced Establishment media, led by *Time*'s Hedley Donovan and Trilateral syndicated columnists Joseph Kraft and Carl Rowan.

Major New York Carter backers, who served on the Wall Street Committee for Carter or hosted gatherings on his behalf, included Roger C. Altman, partner of Lehman Brothers, the chairman of which, Peter G. Peterson, was a Trilateral member; banker John Bowles; C. Douglas Dillon, of Dillon, Read, who also served as a member of the international advisory board of the Chase Manhattan Bank; and Cyrus Vance, a Trilateral founder and vice-chairman of the CFR.

Furthermore, of the six national finance directors of Jimmy Carter's costly pre-convention race for the Presidential nomination, three were high officials at Lehman Brothers, one was a vice-president of Paine, Webber, another was a vice-president of Kidder, Peabody, and a sixth was the venerable John L. Loeb, senior partner of Loeb, Rhodes, & Co., and a Lehman by marriage. Other prominent business fundraisers for Carter's election campaign included Walter Rothschild, who had married a member of the Warburg family of Kuhn, Loeb & Co., and Felix Rohatyn, a partner of Lazard Frères.

The Carter administration proved to be Trilateral through and through, especially in foreign affairs. Trilateral members holding high posts in the Carter administration included:

- President, James Earl Carter;
- Vice-President, Walter ("Fritz") Mondale;
- National Security Adviser, Zbigniew Brzezinski;
- Secretary of State, Cyrus Vance, who was now chairman of the board of the Rockefeller Foundation. Vance's law firm of Simpson, Thacher & Bartlett had long served as general counsel for Lehman Brothers and Manufacturers Hanover Trust Co. Vance himself served up to 1977 as a director of IBM, the New York Times Co., and Lehman's One William Street Fund. It perhaps also helped Vance's cause that Simpson, Thacher & Bartlett was the New York general counsel for Coca-Cola Co.
- Deputy Secretary of State, Warren Christopher. This Los Angeles corporate lawyer had no diplomatic experience whatever for this high post, but his law firm of O'Melveny and Myers was a prominent one, and he acted as the Los Angeles attorney for IBM. More important was the fact that Christopher was the only Trilateral Commission member from the Western half of the United States.

- Under-Secretary of State for Economic Affairs, Richard Cooper. This Yale professor was also on the board of the Rockefeller-controlled J. Henry Schroder Banking Corporation.
- Under-Secretary of State for Security Assistance, Science, and Technology, Lucy Wilson Benson. Mrs. Benson had been a longtime president of the League of Women Votes and highly active in Common Cause; she was also a board member of the Lehman-oriented Federated Department Stores.
- Assistant Secretary of State for East Asian and Pacific Affairs, Richard Holbrooke.
- Ambassador at Large, Henry D. Owen, of the Brookings institution and the CFR.
- Ambassador at Large for the Law of the Sea Treaty, Elliot Richardson.
- Ambassador at Large for Non-Proliferation Matters (nuclear weapons negotiations), Gerald C. Smith, head of the U.S. delegation at the SALT talks under Nixon, Washington attorney at Wilmer, Cutler & Pickering, and North American Chairman of the Trilateral Commission.
- Ambassador to the United Nations, Andrew Young.
- Chief Disarmament Negotiator, Paul C. Warnke, senior partner of Clark Clifford's influential Washington law firm.
- Assistant Secretary of the Treasury for International Affairs, C. Fred Bergsten, of the Brookings Institution, consultant to the Rockefeller Foundation, and a member of the editorial board of the CFR's prestigious quarterly journal, *Foreign Affairs*.
- Ambassador to Communist China, Leonard Woodcock, formerly head of the United Automobile Workers. It is interesting to note that it was under the Carter-Woodcock aegis that, one week after the first establishment of formal ambassadorial relations with Communist China, China signed an agreement with Coca-Cola giving it exclusive cola sales in that country.

- Secretary of Defense, Harold Brown. This physicist was president of the California Institute of Technology — the only Trilateral college president — and also served on the board of IBM and of Schroders, Ltd., the Rockefeller-controlled British parent company of J. Henry Schroder Bank of New York.
- Deputy to the Director of the CIA, Harvard Professor Robert R. Bowie.
- Secretary of the Treasury, W. Michael Blumenthal, head of Bendix Corp., a director of the CFR, and a trustee of the Rockefeller Foundation.
- Chairman of the Federal Reserve Board, Paul A. Volcker. Volcker was named chairman by President Carter at the suggestion of David Rockefeller. Small wonder, since Volcker had been an executive at the Chase Manhattan Bank, and was a director of the CFR and a trustee of the Rockefeller Foundation.
- And finally, White House Advisor on Domestic and Foreign Policy, Hedley Donovan, formerly editor-in-chief of *Time* magazine.

One of the first important Carter foreign policy actions was the negotiation of the Panama Canal treaty, giving the Canal to Panama, and settling the controversy in such a way that U.S. taxpayers paid millions of dollars to the Panama government so they could repay their very heavy loans to a number of Wall Street banks.

One co-negotiator of the treaty was Ellsworth Bunker, who had been engaged in fruitless negotiations since 1974. The treaty was not concluded until Carter added as co-negotiator the Trilateralist Sol Linowitz, a senior Washington partner of the Wall Street corporate law firm of Coudert Brothers, and a board member of Pan-Am Airways, the Marine Midland Bank of New York, and Time, Inc.

The Marine Midland Bank itself held part of two bank consortium loans to Panama. Furthermore, no fewer than 32 Trilaterals were on the boards of the 31 banks participating in a $115 million

10-year Eurodollar Panama loan issued in 1972; and 15 Trilaterals were on the boards of fourteen banks participating in the $20 million Panama promissory note issued in the same year.

Another crucial foreign policy action of the Carter regime was the President's reluctant decision to admit the Shah of Iran into the U.S., a decision that led directly to the Iran hostage crisis and the freezing of Iranian assets in the U.S. Carter was pressured into this move by the persistent lobbying of David Rockefeller and Henry Kissinger, who might well have realized that a hostage crisis would ensue. As a result, Iran was prevented from pursuing its threat of taking its massive deposits out of Chase Manhattan Bank, which would have caused Chase a great deal of financial difficulty. In politics, one hand washes the other.

Kissinger, by the way, was scarcely put back in the shadows when he left government office in 1977. He quickly became a director of the CFR, a member of the executive committee of the Trilateral Commission, and chairman of the International Advisory Board of the Chase Manhattan Bank.

While Ronald Reagan's early campaigning included attacks on the Trilateral Commission, the Trilateralists have by now been assured that the Reagan administration is in safe hands.

The signal was Reagan's choice of Trilateralist George Bush, who had also become a director of the First International Bank of London and Houston, as Vice-President of the United States, and of Reagan's post-convention reconciliation visit to Washington and to the home of David Rockefeller.

Reagan's most influential White House aides, like James A. Baker, had been top campaigners for Bush for President in 1980. The most influential corporate firm in the Reagan administration is the California-based Bechtel Corporation. Bechtel vice-president and general counsel Caspar Weinberger, a Trilateralist, is Secretary of Defense, and fellow top Bechtel executive George Shultz, former board member of Borg-Warner Corp., General American Transportation Corp., and Stein, Roe & Farnham Balanced Fund, is Secretary of State.

Trilateralist Arthur F. Burns, former Chairman of the Fed, is ambassador to West Germany, Paul Volcker has been reappointed as head of the Fed, and Henry Kissinger is at least partially back as head of a Presidential Commission to study the question of Central America.

It is hard to see how the Trilateralists can lose in the 1984 elections. On the Republican ticket they have George Bush, the heir apparent to Ronald Reagan; and in the Democratic race the two front-runners, Walter Mondale and John Glenn, are both Trilateralists, as is Alan Cranston of California. And, as a long shot, John Anderson of the "National Unity Party" is also a Trilateral member. To paraphrase a famous statement by White House aide Jack Valenti about Lyndon Johnson, the Trilateralists and the financial power elite can sleep well at night regardless of who wins in 1984.

Bibliography

Burch, Jr., Philip H. *Elites in American History*, Volume 2: *From the Civil War to the New Deal.* New York: Holmes and Meier, 1981.

Chernow, Ron. *The House of Morgan: An American Banking Dynasty and the Rise of Modern Finance.* New York: Atlantic Monthly Press, 1990.

Domhoff, G. William. *The Power Elite and the State: How Power Is Made in America.* New York: Aldine de Gruyter, 1990.

Etherington, Norman. *Theories of Imperialism: War, Conquest, and Capital.* Totowa, N.J.: Barnes and Noble, 1984.

Ferguson, Thomas. *Golden Rule: The Investment Theory of Party Competition and the Logic of Money-Driven Political Systems.* Chicago: University of Chicago, 1995.

George, Alexander L., and Juliette L. George. *Woodrow Wilson and Colonel House: A Personality Study.* New York: The John Day Company, 1956.

Grinder, Walter E., and John Hagel, III. "Toward a Theory of State Capitalism: Ultimate Decision-Making and Class Structure." *Journal of Libertarian Studies* 1, no. 1 (1977): 59–79.

Kolko. Gabriel. *The Triumph of Conservatism: A Reinterpretation of American History.* Glencoe, Ill.: The Free Press, 1983.

Livingston, James. *Origins of the Federal Reserve System: Money, Class, and Corporate Capitalism, 1890–1913.* Ithaca, N.Y.: Cornell University Press, 1986.

Quigley, Carroll. *The Anglo-American Establishment: From Rhodes to Cliveden.* New York: Books in Focus, 1981.

———. *Tragedy and Hope: A History of the World in Our Time.* New York: Macmillan, 1966.

Rothbard, Murray N. *The Case Against the Fed.* Auburn, Ala.: Ludwig von Mises Institute, 2008.

———. *History of Money and Banking in the United States: From the Colonial Era to World War II.* Auburn, Ala.: Ludwig von Mises Institute, 1982.

Shoup, Laurence H., and William Minter. *Imperial Brain Trust: The Council on Foreign Relations and United States Foreign Policy.* Monthly Review Press, 1977.

Tansill Charles C. *America Goes to War.* Boston: Little, Brown and Company, 1938.

Weinstein, James. *The Corporate Ideal in the Liberal State, 1900–1918.* Boston: Beacon Press, 1968

Williams, William A. *The Tragedy of American Diplomacy.* Cleveland, Ohio: World Publishing, 1959.

Index